A Mind for Math

Genesis Curriculum
The Book of Matthew

First Edition

Welcome to *A Mind for Math*, part of Genesis Curriculum. Its focus is on thinking about how to use math to answer questions and how numbers work together and can be manipulated. Parents are the teachers and should be comfortable with arithmetic. There are not many examples in the children's workbooks. There are examples and walkthrough problems in this book which is the lesson guide and answer key. I use mental math techniques to teach kids how to work with numbers. Please teach them to your kids, but you can also show them other methods of attempting problems. I recommend waiting until they get the mental math way first. Then kids can decide what they like best when they do the end of the year review. Kids who already know the traditional methods can use them, but introduce them to the mental math tricks as they may find them easier. Mental math methods make problems easier by breaking them down into more manageable parts.

This course is done like those in the main curriculum. It draws on the daily Bible reading. To use the curriculum, you just read through the lesson from the beginning. It will give a little summary of the Matthew reading that I used for the main curriculum lesson. Stop and let them answer questions before moving on.

They can work out answers in their leveled workbooks. There are four different workbooks: levels A, B, C, D. Each leveled workbook has its own problems and those for the levels before it. There can be more questions in the lesson than in their workbooks; those can be answered orally. The student workbooks also don't have the hints that are in the lessons.

Everyone can walk through the lessons together. I let my older son tell his younger brother if he got a problem correct or not, and he helped him out if he was stuck. It built my older son's confidence tremendously, which was a goal in making this. Getting numerous problems correct before trying the problems on his own level made him not only willing to do his work, but even eager at times, instead of trying to avoid math.

By working with the older kids, younger kids will get exposed to more advanced concepts, and the older kids will get daily review by working with the younger children. You can even use the higher levels to challenge a younger kid who is eager to try more.

On review days they will be working on their own problems in their own workbooks. There are 180 days of work in their workbooks. When the main curriculum breaks at 140 days, the math books have individual review pages for the remaining 40 days. That means you don't have to gather each day for a lesson, but they can keep going with their math, which is really good for them instead of taking a big break from it and losing a lot of progress.

This book covers math for elementary students, about grades one through four. The fifth/sixth grade course in Easy Peasy starts at 1 + 1 and works up, so it's a good course to follow this curriculum since it will make sure there are no gaps.

It would be nice to have available a ruler with inches and centimeters, a die for a lesson, coins, and blocks like cube building blocks of Duplos which can be used for many things like dividing into groups. Those are mentioned in parentheses next to the day number where they are used. You should also know that in the back of the book there is a list of topics covered by day and by level.

Students should be working on math facts every day apart from the curriculum. They are expected to use addition and subtraction facts in levels A and B, multiplication in level C, and division in level D. They can use daily facts practice sheets (which GC has in books or on our site to print for free) and facts games to get daily exposure. If your child doesn't know the facts necessary, they can still use their appropriate level. They can use counting, draw their own number line to use, look up facts in their fact practice books, etc. to help them out.

Day 1

A: Counting Backwards, Ordinals B: Critical Thinking C: Multiple Addends

The beginning of the genealogy list of Jesus' ancestors. (Matthew 1:1-11)

A.   There are about twenty-five fathers listed in the genealogy list. It's tracing back from Jesus who his ancestors were. Count backwards from twenty-five.

Check in your workbook for a list of names. Who is first? Who is tenth? Who is third in line? Write those ordinal numbers with numbers instead of words.

first: Abraham, tenth: Salmon, third: Jacob, 1st, 10th, 3rd

B.   Think about this. If each of the twenty-five fathers had two children, how many children would they have all together? What about if they each had four children? (Hint: Four is double two, so their answer will be double.) Count by 25s.

50, 100, 25-50-75-100-125-150-175-200-225-250-275-300....

C.   Let's say that each of the twenty-five fathers had sixteen sons. How many sons did they have all together? How would you figure that out?

That's 25 sixteen times. You don't know how to multiply like that yet, so what can you do? You already figured out 2 children and 4 children. What's the relationship between 16 and 4 or how can you get from four to sixteen? 16 is 4 x 4. So this answer will be four times the answer of 4 children each, which was 100. What's 100 four times? 100 + 100 + 100 + 100 = 400

Remember that 1 times any number is itself. 4 x 1 = 4
When you multiply by zeros in a number, you just ignore them and then tag them back on. Here's an example.

4 x 100 = 4 x 1 with two zeros = 4 with two zeros = 400

Let's say that Abraham lived to be 127, Isaac to 118, and Jacob to 109. How long did they lived combined?

354
You can combine the hundreds, tens, and ones separately.
127 = 100 + 20 + 7 and 118 = 100 + 10 + 8 and 109 = 100 + 9
127 + 118 + 109 = 100 + 100 + 100 + 20 + 10 + 7 + 8 + 9 = 300 + 30 + 24 = 354

D. Let's say each of the twenty-five fathers lived to be 100. How many years did they live combined?

25 x 100 = 2500 years

Let's say that Abraham lived to be 117, Isaac to 108, and Jacob to 99, Judah to 115, and Perez to 120. How long did they lived combined?

559
117 = 100 + 10 + 7 and 108 = 100 + 8 and 99 = 90 + 9 and 115 = 100 + 10 + 5 and 120 = 100 + 20
117 + 108 + 99 + 115 + 120 =
100 + 100 + 100 + 100 + 10 + 90 + 10 + 20 + 7 + 8 + 9 + 5 = 400 + 130 + 29 = 559

Day 2
A: Skip counting by 2, 5 C: Multiplication

This is the list of Jesus' ancestors up through when Jesus is born. (Matthew 1:12-25)

A.   If a new relative of Jesus was born every two years, how many new relatives would He have after ten years? If he had a new relative born every five years, how many new relatives would Jesus have after twenty years?

5 new relatives – Skip count by twos to ten while counting on your fingers or making tally marks. Each time you say a number a new relative is born. After two years there is 1 new relative. After four years there is 1 more new relative. That makes 2 so far. Continue until you get to ten years.

4 new relatives – Skip count by fives to twenty. Count on your fingers or make a tally mark for each number you say. Every time you say a number a new baby is born. ☺

Can you start at 34 and count by twos? Can you start at 33 and count by twos?

34, 36, 38, 40, 42, …   33, 35, 37, 39, 41, 43, …

Can you start at 65 and count by fives?

65, 70, 75, 80, 85, 90,…

B.   It says there were fourteen generations from Abraham to David and from David to the deportation. How many generations is that in all? How many more generations would there be until there were thirty?

14 + 14 = 28 generations, 2 generations	14
They can write these vertically and add them straight up and down.	+14
1 + 1 = 2 and 4 + 4 = 8	28

If there were two more generations until it reached thirty, how many more generations until it reached forty? How many to reach fifty? (Note: There's a hundreds chart on Day 7 that they can refer to and see how the ones stay the same as you jump ten more on the chart.)

12 generations, 22 generations

C.   There were also fourteen generations from the deportation until the Messiah. That's three sets of fourteen generations. How many generations is that?

42 = 14 + 14 + 14 = 10 + 10 + 10 + 4 + 4 + 4 = 30 + 12
   Fourteen breaks apart into ten and four.

If there had been 7 generations between each instead of 14, how many would there have been all together? (In other words, how many generations if there had been three sets of seven generations?) What if there had been three sets of eight generations each? What if there had been four sets of six generations each?

21, 24, 24 (This is just 7 x 3, 8 x 3, and 4 x 6.)

D.   Use multiplication to find the answer of three sets of fourteen generations.

42 = 14 x 3 = 10 x 3 and 4 x 3 = 30 and 12 = 30 + 12

What if it had been 14 generations seven times?

98 = 14 x 7 = 10 x 7 and 4 x 7 = 70 + 28

What if it had been 26 generations for each of the three sets?

78 = 26 x 3 = 20 x 3 and 6 x 3 = 60 + 18

Day 3

Time

Herod wanted to determine the exact time the star appeared. (Matthew 2:1-12)

A.   When you read a digital clock, the first number is the hour. The number after the colon, the dots, is how many minutes it has been after the hour. Read the times on the clocks.

one o'clock, twelve o'clock, nine thirty, two thirty

Thirty minutes is half an hour, and the AM after 9:30 means before noon. Noon is what we call twelve o'clock in the middle of the day. So does the clock say nine thirty in the morning or nine thirty at night? **morning** The PM next to two thirty means after noon. So does that clock say that it's two thirty in the morning or two thirty in the afternoon? **afternoon** (Note: The AM and PM stand for Latin words that just literally mean before and after midday.)

B.   When you read an analog clock, first you look for what number the hour hand is pointing to or that it comes after. The hour hand is the shorter line. What hour would you read on these clocks?

three and eight

You can show your child how the hour hand on the second clock is halfway between the eight and the nine because the minute hand has gone halfway around the clock. As the minute hand keeps going and gets closer and closer to the top, the hour hand gets closer and closer to the next hour.

How many minutes is halfway around the clock? (Hint: They just learned how many minutes were in half an hour.)

30 minutes

This is how you read the clocks. The first clock reads three o'clock because the minute hand is at zero. No minutes have gone by past the hour. The second one reads eight thirty. Thirty minutes have gone by since it was eight o'clock.

Every number on the clock marks when five minutes have passed. Put your finger on the twelve and count by fives around the clock. You should get to thirty when you reach the six, halfway around the clock. Keep counting all the way around to find how many minutes is an hour, which is all the way around the clock?

60 minutes

What time does this clock say?

eleven thirty

C.   Read these clocks.

nine forty-five, three thirty, one fifty-five
For the last one it's almost two, so this is tricky. They have to notice that the minute hand is almost to the hour, so the hour hand is going to be almost to the hour.

D.   What does each number on the clock show?

the hours and marks every five minutes

What does each little line between the numbers show? They show each minute. If there were a second hand on the clock, they would show each second that's gone by as well.

Read these clocks to the nearest minute. The extra line there that's thinner than the others is the second hand.

7:11, 8:07

We would most naturally read that second time as eight O seven.

Day 4
Addition

Joseph had to take Mary and Jesus to Egypt. (Matthew 2:13-21)

A.   Let's say that Joseph and his family traveled 6 miles and then 2 miles more. How far did they travel?

8 miles

If they went another 2 miles, how far would it be then?

10 miles

What if they went another 10 miles? What's ten plus ten? Use your fingers to count on from ten if you don't know.

20 miles
Ten plus ten is just like counting by ten two times.

B.   If Joseph and his family had to travel 8 miles and then went another 7 miles, how far would they have traveled?

15 miles

What if they went an extra 5 miles? How far would that be all together? Count by fives to add five onto fifteen.

20 miles

What if they went yet another twenty miles? How far would that be all together?

40 miles

C.   If Joseph and his family traveled 31 miles and then another 24 miles, how far did they travel all together? Break it apart to add.

55 miles (31 is 30 and 1. 24 is 20 and 4. 31 + 24 = 30 + 20 and 1 + 4 = 50 and 5)

If they traveled another 12 miles, how far would they have traveled all together?

67 miles (55 is 50 and 5. 12 is 10 and 2. To add them you add 50 + 10 and 5 + 2.
That's 60 and 7 or 67.)

If they went 25 more miles, how far would they have traveled all together?

92 miles (67 is 60 and 7. 25 is 20 and 5. 67 + 32 = 60 + 20 and 7 + 5 = 80 and 12)

D.   If Joseph and his family went 24 miles and then 67 miles, how far did they go all together?

91 miles (24 + 67 = 20 + 60 and 4 + 7 = 80 and 11 = 91)

If they went another 48 miles, how far would they have traveled all together?

139 miles (91 + 48 = 90 + 40 and 1 + 8 = 130 and 9 = 139)

If they went another 35 miles, how far would they have traveled all together?

174 miles (139 + 35 = 100 + 30 + 30 + 9 + 5 = 100 + 60 + 14 = 174)

Day 5
Review

A.   Abraham, Isaac, Jacob, and Judah were Jesus' first ancestors listed in his Matthew genealogy. Who was fourth in line?

Judah

Skip count to fill in the blanks.

6   8   10   **12**   14   16   18   20   22   **24**

5   10   15   **20**   25   30   35   40   45   **50**

Which clock says three o'clock?

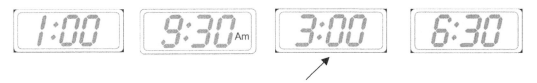

Do you eat breakfast in the AM or PM?

AM

If Joseph and his family traveled 4 miles, then 2 miles, then 3 miles, and then 1 mile, how far did they go all together?

10 miles

B.   Skip count by 25 to fill in the blanks.

25   50   **75**   100   125   **150**   175   200

Add.

15	23	31
+ 12	+ 45	+ 24
27	**68**	**55**

What time do these clocks say?

one, two thirty

If Joseph and his family traveled 4 miles, 6 miles, 7miles, and then 12 miles, how far did they travel all together?

29 miles

C.   What's four times two hundred?

800

Add: 24 + 135 = **159**   Add: 106 + 117 = **223**

Find the sum: 35 + 67 + 123 = **225**

Multiply: 8 x 6 = **48**   5 x 7 = **35**   9 x 3 = **27**   7 x 8 = **56**

Read this clock.

1:55

D. Add: 157 + 105 + 206 + 129 = **597**

Find the sum: 112 + 260 + 328 = **700**

Multiply: 34 x 200 = **6800**

Multiply: 15 x 5 = **75**

23 x 7 = **161**

What time does the clock say?

   **10:11**

Day 6
Multiple Addends D: Multiplication

Jesus is going to gather the wheat into the barn. (Matthew 3:11-17)

A.   Jesus isn't really going to gather wheat, that's a metaphor. It's talking about gathering the believers to the home He's prepared for them in heaven. But for today, let's talk about gathering wheat into the barn.

If 5 bushels of wheat and then 3 bushels of wheat and then 7 bushels of wheat were gathered, how many would have been gathered in all?

15 bushels

Now try with these numbers: 4 and 5 and 9, 3 and 4 and 6, 2 and 7 and 8.

18 bushels, 13 bushels, 17 bushels

B.   If 8 bushels and 7 bushels and 4 more bushels were gathered, how many were gathered all together?

19 bushels

Now try it with these numbers: 9 and 6 and 4, 5 and 8 and 4, 3 and 8 and 7.

19 bushels, 17 bushels, 18 bushels

C.   If 24 bushels, 31 bushels, and 111 bushels were gathered, how many were gathered all together?

166 bushels 24 is 20 and 4. 31 is 30 and 1. 111 is 100 and 10 and 1. Add the parts together: $100 + 20 + 30 + 10 + 4 + 1 + 1 = 100 + 60 + 6 = 166$

Now try with these numbers: 9 bushels 4 times, 7 bushels 7 times, 240 and 35 and 17 bushels.

36 bushels, 49 bushels, 292 bushels

D.   If 57 bushels were gathered 3 times, how many were gathered all together?

171 bushels
57 is 50 and 7.
57 x 3 is 50 x 3 and 7 x 3 = 150 + 21 = 171
50 x 3 = 5 x 3 x 10 = 15 with a zero tagged on, 150

Now try with these numbers: 26 bushels 6 times, 19 bushels 5 times, 35 bushels 8 times.

156 bushels, 95 bushels, 280 bushels

Day 7
A: Using a hundred's chart B: Multiplication

Jesus went into the wilderness for forty days and forty nights. (Matthew 4:1-11)

A.   How much is that all together? We're going to use a chart to figure it out.

1	2	3	4	5	6	7	8	9	10
11	12	13	14	15	16	17	18	19	20
21	22	23	24	25	26	27	28	29	30
31	32	33	34	35	36	37	38	39	40
41	42	43	44	45	46	47	48	49	50
51	52	53	54	55	56	57	58	59	60
61	62	63	64	65	66	67	68	69	70
71	72	73	74	75	76	77	78	79	80
81	82	83	84	85	86	87	88	89	90
91	92	93	94	95	96	97	98	99	100

Can you make observations about the chart? Every line is ten numbers. If you move over one square to the right, you are counting up one number. If you move over one square to the left, you are counting backward one number. If you jump down one line, you are adding on ten or counting by ten. 11 to 21 to 31 to 41 is counting by tens, just starting with 11 instead of 10.

Put your finger on four and count up four, jumping to the right one box each time you say a number. You should end up on 8, the answer to 4 + 4. You started at four and went four more.

Put your finger on fourteen and count up four, jumping box to box with each number. Did you land on 18? Fourteen plus four is eighteen. If not, try again.

Now put your finger on the 10 and count to 40 by tens. Jump down a line each time. Now do it again from where you are on 40 and count on 40 more by counting by tens. Keep jumping down the chart with each number (ten, twenty, thirty, forty). Did you land on eighty? If not, try again.

What's 40 + 40? **80**

Use the chart to find the answers.

30 + 30 = **60**   20 + 20 = **40**

24 + 4 = **28**   42 + 2 = **44**

B.   How many days and nights all together is forty days and forty nights?

80 days and nights

What if he went for another forty days and forty nights? This is 80 doubled or two times. To multiply something by two we just double it, or add it to itself.

160 days
80 plus 80 is just 8 plus 8 with a zero tagged on. You can also write the numbers vertically and just add straight down.

How many times did we add forty to get to 160 days?

4 times
40 days + 40 nights + 40 days + 40 nights

Adding forty four times is the same as multiplying 40 times 4. We write that 40 x 4. We can add to multiply, but when you learn your multiplication facts, you can multiply to find the answer faster.

What's **20 x 4**? That's just four two times with a zero tagged on.

80

C.   If He spent forty days and forty nights in the wilderness six times, how many days and nights is that all together?

480 days and nights
That's 40 + 40 multiplied by 6. To multiply 80 x 6 we just multiply 8 x 6 and then tag on the zero.

If He spent 40 days and 40 nights 7 times or 8 times or 9 times, how many days and nights would that be?

560 days and nights, 640 days and nights, 720 days and nights

D.   How many hours is 40 days and 40 nights?

960 hours
This is 24 x 40 = 20 and 4 times 4 with a zero.
20 x 4 and 4 x 4 = 80 and 16 = 96 Then tag on the zero from the 40. This is just like multiplying by ten. 40 is 4 x 10. So, the answer is 960.

Your child could also think of 24 x 40 as 12 x 80 (12 x 2 x 40). It's really easy to multiply by 12 since it's just multiplying by 10 and 2. Realizing how you can break apart numbers and manipulate them can make math easier and more interesting and meaningful.

How many hours is 30 days and 30 nights? What about 60 days and nights? What about 70 days and nights?

720 hours, 1440 hours, 1680 hours

Think! Why is the answer for 60 days and nights double the answer for 30 days and nights? Why is the answer for 70 days and nights 240 more than for 60 days and nights?

60 is double 30, so the answer is doubled. 240 hours is ten days or 24 x 10. To find 80 days and nights, you could just add 240 more hours to the answer for 70 days because you're just adding the hours for ten days.

Day 8
Subtraction

Jesus left Capernaum and went into Galilee. (Matthew 4:12-22)

A. If Jesus had 16 miles to walk and had gone 8 so far, how many miles would he need to go to get to Galilee? (Hint: If they don't know how to figure out the answer, have them draw a picture. Just draw a line. One end of the line is where He begins and the other end is 16 miles away, where Jesus needs to get to. Move your finger along the line about halfway. That's where He is now, 8 miles into His 16-mile trip. How much is left? They need to think what plus 8 equals 16, which is easiest done with subtraction. 16 – 8 =)

8 miles

Now try with these numbers: 7 miles into a 13 mile trip, 5 miles into a 14 mile trip, 9 miles into a 12 mile trip

6 miles, 9 miles, 3 miles

B. If Jesus had a 64 mile trip and had gone 20 miles so far, how far would He still have to go? (Hint: They can write the problems vertically, just like with addition, and subtract straight up and down.)

44 miles

Now try with these numbers: 13 miles into a 55 mile trip, 24 miles into a 76 mile trip, 40 miles into a 90 mile trip.

42 miles, 52 miles, 50 miles

C.   If Jesus had a 34 mile trip and had gone 25 miles so far, how much farther would He need to go? You are going to break these apart to subtract just like you would break apart an addition problem.

Break apart 34 into 30 and 4 and 25 into 20 and 5. Then subtract the parts.
30 – 20 and 4 – 5
30 – 20 = 10 but what is 4 – 5? Use the number line to find out. Start at the 4 and count down 5. What's the answer? **- 1**

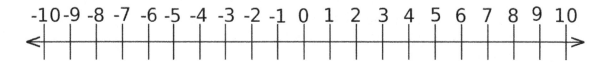

If I had to pay you five dollars and I only had four so I gave you those, how much money would I still owe you? **$1** But I don't have a dollar. I need to show that it's a dollar I owe. It's like I have negative one dollars because as soon as I get a dollar, I'm going to have to give it to you. We write negative one with a minus sign, - 1.

So back to our answer. Jesus still needs to walk 10 and - 1 miles. What's that? It's just 10 – 1. That negative sign is just a minus sign. They are the same thing. What's 10 – 1? 9

9 miles

Try it with these numbers: 26 miles into a 35 mile trip, 33 miles into a 41 mile trip, 53 miles into a 62 mile trip.

9 miles, 8 miles, 9 miles

D.   If Jesus was 58 miles into an 82 mile trip, how much farther does He have to walk?

24 miles

Now try it with these numbers: 38 miles into a 93 mile trip, 67 miles into a 84 mile trip, 49 miles into a 75 mile trip.

55 miles, 17 miles, 26 miles

Day 9 (cubes, square blocks)
Area

News of Jesus spread throughout all of Syria. (Matthew 4:23-25)

A.   If news of Jesus spread throughout all of Syria, how far and wide did news of Him spread? To figure that out we need to find the area of Syria, how much land there is there. We're not going to really measure the country of Syria, but let's figure out different areas. Get out 12 blocks or draw 12 blocks in three rows of four. What's the area of the bigger block you made with them all together?

12 blocks

What happens if you arrange the blocks in 1 row of 12 blocks or 2 rows of 6 blocks or 4 rows of 3 blocks? What is the area in those cases?

It's still 12 blocks each time. No matter the shape of it, it was still made of the same twelve blocks.

B.   Now get out 20 blocks or draw them. In how many ways can you make a shape with an area of 20 blocks?

So many! It doesn't have to be a regular shape. It could look like the letter T, whatever you want, as long as they are all touching and all twenty blocks are used.

C.   The area of the rectangle that was made by 3 rows of 4 blocks was 12. Three rows of four is just like four three times. To find the area we multiply the amount in each row by the number of rows. Three times four equals twelve. What would be the area of a rectangle that is four blocks in each row with five rows?

20 blocks

What's the area of these rectangles? Six rows of seven, eight rows of three, nine rows of four

42 blocks, 24 blocks, 36 blocks

D.   The official formula for the area of a rectangle is length times width. What would the area be of rectangles with the following lengths and widths: length 12 and width 5, length 17 and width 4, length 27 and width 8
60, 68, 216

Day 10
Review

A.   What if 4 bushels of wheat and then 5 bushels of wheat and then 7 bushels of wheat were gathered? How many would have been gathered in all?

16 bushels

Use the chart to figure out twenty plus thirty and twelve plus three.

50, 15

1	2	3	4	5	6	7	8	9	10
11	12	13	14	15	16	17	18	19	20
21	22	23	24	25	26	27	28	29	30
31	32	33	34	35	36	37	38	39	40
41	42	43	44	45	46	47	48	49	50
51	52	53	54	55	56	57	58	59	60
61	62	63	64	65	66	67	68	69	70
71	72	73	74	75	76	77	78	79	80
81	82	83	84	85	86	87	88	89	90
91	92	93	94	95	96	97	98	99	100

If Jesus had 15 miles to walk and had gone 7 miles so far, how many miles would He need to go to get where He was going?

8 miles

Add: $5 + 7 =$ $6 + 9 =$ $4 + 6 =$ $3 + 8 =$ $6 + 8 =$
    12   **15**   **10**   **11**   **14**

B.   What if 8 bushels and 5 bushels and 4 more bushels were gathered? How many were gathered all together?

17 bushels

Double 70.

140
70 plus 70 is just 7 plus 7 with a zero tagged on. You can also write the numbers vertically and just add straight down.

If Jesus had a 76 mile trip and had gone 40 miles so far, how far would He still have to go?

36 miles

Subtract: 35 – 20, 67 – 41, 89 – 25

15, 26, 64

C.   What if 123 bushels, 41 bushels, and 54 bushels were gathered? How many were gathered all together?

218 bushels
123 + 41 + 54 = 100 + 20 + 40 + 50 + 3 + 1 + 4 = 100 + 110 + 8 = 218

What is thirty times six? What is sixty times eight?

180, 480
To multiply 30 x 6 we just multiply 3 x 6 and then tag on the zero.

What would be the area of a rectangle that is seven blocks in a row with six rows?

42 blocks

Subtract: 42 – 16, 63 – 24, 41 – 12, 37 – 29
          26   39   29   8

D.   If 48 bushels were gathered 6 times, how many were gathered all together?

288 bushels
48 x 6 = 40 x 6 and 8 x 6 = 240 + 48 = 288

How many hours is 30 days?

720 hours
This is 24 x 30 which is 24 x 3 with a zero tagged onto the answer.
20 x 3 and 4 x 3 = 60 + 12 = 72 Then multiply by ten because it was 30 we were multiplying by not three. To multiply by ten we just need to tag on a zero.

If Jesus was 47 miles into a 92 mile trip, how much farther does He have to walk?

45 miles

What would the area be of a rectangle width of 7 and a length of 34?

238 = 7 x 34

Day 11
Subtraction

Tasteless salt is good for nothing except to be tossed out. (Matthew 5:13-20).

A.   We're going to throw away tasteless salt today for math. If you had 40 pounds of salt and had to throw away ten pounds of it, how many pounds would be left? Use the chart. Put your finger on the forty. Which way would you jump to subtract ten? Will your answer be more or less than forty?

Your answer will be less than forty, so you need to jump upwards on the chart, toward the top of the page. You are jumping back ten numbers. You can jump block to block and count back ten, or you can just jump from forty to thirty. Each line is ten blocks, so you can jump up one row to find the number that is ten before.

1	2	3	4	5	6	7	8	9	10
11	12	13	14	15	16	17	18	19	20
21	22	23	24	25	26	27	28	29	30
31	32	33	34	35	36	37	38	39	40
41	42	43	44	45	46	47	48	49	50
51	52	53	54	55	56	57	58	59	60
61	62	63	64	65	66	67	68	69	70
71	72	73	74	75	76	77	78	79	80
81	82	83	84	85	86	87	88	89	90
91	92	93	94	95	96	97	98	99	100

Make observations about subtracting it vertically.

$$\begin{array}{r} 40 \\ -\ 10 \\ \hline 30 \end{array}$$

Can you see $4 - 1 = 3$ and $0 - 0 = 0$? (Note: We'll be learning about this in coming weeks. We're not there yet.)

Now subtract these numbers: $50 - 20$, $60 - 40$, $80 - 30$, $90 - 20$

30, 20, 50, 70

B.	What if we had 46 kilograms of salt and had to throw away 20 kilograms of it? Use the chart and jump two rows to find the answer.

46
- 20
26   You can see this as 4 – 2 and 6 – 0.

Now subtract these numbers: 82 – 50, 78 – 20, 95 – 45, 36 - 23

32, 58, 50, 13

C.	What if we had 45 ounces of salt and had to throw 8 ounces away? That's forty minus nothing and five minus eight. What's five minus eight? **negative 3** So, take 3 away from 40. You can count backwards or just think about 10 minus 3.

45
- 8
40
- 3
37

Now subtract these numbers: 52 – 25, 45 – 37, 81 – 53, 64 – 17
27, 8, 28, 47

D.	What if we had 451 grams of salt and had to throw away 360 grams of it? Break it up to subtract. What are the pieces? **400 – 300, 50 – 60, 1 – 0**

451
- 360   You could subtract everything straight down that's not negative.
100   101
- 10   - 10
+ 1   91   The important thing is understanding you are taking away
91   hundreds, tens, and ones, and they can be done separately.

Now subtract these numbers. 508 – 215, 417 – 233, 574 – 256, 450 – 315
Remember that when you are subtracting off of 200, the answer is 100 something. If you are subtracting from 300, the answer will be 200 something, etc.

293, 184, 318, 135

Day 12 (ten one-dollar bills, or ten pieces of paper, or pretend money)
Dividing

They will have to pay to their debt to the very last cent. (Matthew 5:21-26)

A.   Oh no! We have a debt to pay. Let's pay it off right away because we don't want
        to be in debt. Let's say that we owe $10 in debt. How many days would it take to
        pay it off if you paid back $1 a day? You can use your money or pretend money
        and pay it back and count the days.

        10 days

        How many days would it take if you paid back two dollars a day? Five dollars a
        day? Ten dollars a day?

        5 days, 2 days, 1 day

B.   Let's get our debt paid off. If you owed $25 dollars, how long would it take for you
        to pay off your debt if you paid back just $1 a day?

        25 days

        What if you paid back five dollars a day? What if you owed $16 dollars and paid
        back four dollars a day? Just $2 a day when you owed $16?

        5 days, 4 days, 8 days

C.   How much money is $2 compared to $4 dollars? **half as much** So, how long does
        it take to pay back the money when you give half as much each day? **It takes twice
        as long.** Use that knowledge to answer these questions.

        If you took fourteen days to pay back your debt, how long would it take you if you
        paid only half as much each day?

        28 days

        If you took twenty days to pay back your debt, how long would it take you if you
        paid twice as much each day? (Think!)

        10 days, half as long

If you owed $18 dollars and paid $3 a day, how long would it take you to pay off your debt?

6 days 3 x 6 = 18 so eighteen divided by three is six.

D.   If you owed $49 and paid back $7 a day, how long would it be before you paid off your debt?

7 days 7 x 7 = 49, 49 ÷ 7 = 7

If you owed $72 and paid back $8 a day, how long would it be before you paid off your debt?

9 days 9 x 8 = 72, 72 ÷ 8 = 9

If you owed $42 and paid it back evenly over six days, how much did you pay back each day?

$7 42 ÷ 6 = 7, 7 x 6 = 42

If you paid back $8 dollars a day for 6 days in order to pay off your debt completely, how much was your debt?

$48 8 x 6 = 48

Day 13
Fractions

You can't turn a hair on your head white or black. (Matthew 5:27-37)

A.   Draw a circle. Pretend that's a head of hair. Color in the whole thing. That's one whole head. Now draw another circle and color in half of it. How much is colored in? Of course, one half, I told you to color in one half. How much is not colored in?

       ½

       Now can you draw another circle and color in half of it in another way?

B.   Draw a circle and pretend that's a head of hair. Divide the head into four quarters by drawing a line to divide it in half and then another line to divide it in half the other way. You should have four sections now. Now think. If you colored in half of the hair the way you did before, how many of the quarters would be colored in?

       2

       Color in half of the hair in a new way. How many ways can you do that? How many ways can you think of? (Note: like a checker board, diagonal quarters instead of ones next to each other)

       Draw one more circle and color in one quarter of it. When one quarter is colored in, how many quarters are not colored in?

       3

C.   Draw a circle and pretend it's a head of hair. Can you color in one third of it? How would you write that as a fraction? The number colored in will go on top and the number of parts goes on the bottom.

       $1/3$

       How many parts of the head of hair aren't colored in? **2** How would you write that as a fraction? (Note: Have them read the fractions out loud.)

       $2/3$

D.   Write one half and one quarter as fractions. How many quarters is one half? (Hint: You already answered this.)

2 quarters

Add one half and one quarter. That's adding 2 quarters and 1 quarter. Draw the answer. Color in two quarters (one half) and one more quarter. How many quarters are colored in? So what's 2 quarters plus 1 quarter? Write the fractions and answer as an equation such as 2 + 1 = 3.

$$\tfrac{1}{2} + \tfrac{1}{4} = \tfrac{2}{4} + \tfrac{1}{4} = \tfrac{3}{4}$$ 2 quarters plus 1 quarter is 3 quarters.

Day 14
Doubling

Jesus said, "Whoever forces you to go one mile, go with him two." (Matthew 5:38-48)

A.   Two miles is twice as far as one mile; it's double the distance. Today we're going to double. What do you need to do to double a number? How do you get from one to two with math?

You add the number to itself to double it. 1 + 1 = 2. One two times is two.

Double these numbers by adding them to themselves. 5, 8, 3, 10, 30 (If you aren't sure about doubling ten and thirty, check your hundred chart for help.)

10, 16, 6, 20, 60

B.   What's twenty-three two times? 23 + 23 = **46** You are multiplying the number by two when you are doubling it. Multiply these numbers by two by doubling them.

31, 14, 44, 32, 50

62, 28, 88, 64, 100

C.   What's double these numbers? 79, 84, 67, 25, 250

158, 168, 134, 50, 500
79 + 79 = 70 + 70 + 9 + 9 = 140 + 18 = 158
250 + 250 = 200 + 200 + 50 + 50 = 400 + 100 = 500

D.   What's double these numbers? 164, 381, 193, 467, 319

328, 762, 386, 934, 638
164 + 164 = 100 + 100 + 60 + 60 + 4 + 4 = 200 + 120 + 8 = 328
386 + 386 = 300 + 300 + 80 + 80 + 6 + 6 = 600 + 160 + 12 = 762
These might be too much for them to do in their heads. They don't have to write all this down. They could skip to writing down one of the steps if they can get the answer from there.

Day 15
Review

A.   Use the hundred chart to subtract 60 – 20 and 50 – 10.

1	2	3	4	5	6	7	8	9	10
11	12	13	14	15	16	17	18	19	20
21	22	23	24	25	26	27	28	29	30
31	32	33	34	35	36	37	38	39	40
41	42	43	44	45	46	47	48	49	50
51	52	53	54	55	56	57	58	59	60
61	62	63	64	65	66	67	68	69	70
71	72	73	74	75	76	77	78	79	80
81	82	83	84	85	86	87	88	89	90
91	92	93	94	95	96	97	98	99	100

40, 40

Let's say that we owe $12 in debt. How many days would it take to pay it off if you paid back $2 a day?

6 days

Draw a circle and divide it in half.

Double these numbers by adding them to themselves. 6, 9, 20

12, 18, 40

B.   Use the chart to subtract these numbers. 40 – 20, 37 – 20

1	2	3	4	5	6	7	8	9	10
11	12	13	14	15	16	17	18	19	20
21	22	23	24	25	26	27	28	29	30
31	32	33	34	35	36	37	38	39	40
41	42	43	44	45	46	47	48	49	50
51	52	53	54	55	56	57	58	59	60
61	62	63	64	65	66	67	68	69	70
71	72	73	74	75	76	77	78	79	80
81	82	83	84	85	86	87	88	89	90
91	92	93	94	95	96	97	98	99	100

```
  40          37
- 20        - 20
  20          17
```

How many days would it take to pay back an $18 loan if you paid back three dollars a day?

6 days

Draw a shape and divide it into quarters.

Multiply these numbers by two by doubling them. 43, 20, 100

86, 40, 200

C. What if we had 42 ounces of salt and had to throw 8 ounces away?

```
  42
-  8
  40
-  6
  34
```

If you owed $24 dollars and paid $4 a day, how long would it take you to pay off your debt?

6 days 4 x 6 = 24 so twenty-four divided by four is six.

Draw a shape and color in two-thirds of it. Write two thirds.

2/3

What's double these numbers? 75, 49, 150

150, 98, 300
75 + 75 = 70 + 70 + 5 + 5 = 140 + 10 = 150
150 + 150 = 100 + 100 + 50 + 50 = 200 + 100 = 300

D. What if we had 324 grams of salt and had to throw away 152 grams of it? How much would be left?

$$324$$
$$- 152$$
$$200$$
$$- 30$$
$$+ 2$$
$$\mathbf{172}$$

If you owed $56 and paid back $7 a day, how long would it be before you paid off your debt?

8 days $7 \times 8 = 56$, $56 \div 7 = 8$

$\frac{1}{2} + \frac{1}{4} = \mathbf{{}^3/_4}$ You can draw a box and divide it into quarters. You can color in half of it and then one more quarter of it to find the answer.

What's double these numbers? 275, 395

550, 790
$275 + 275 = 200 + 200 + 70 + 70 + 5 + 5 = 400 + 140 + 10 = 550$
$395 + 395 = 300 + 300 + 90 + 90 + 5 + 5 = 600 + 180 + 10 = 790$

Day 16
Multiplication

They aren't supposed to use meaningless repetition. (Matthew 6:1-8)

A. We're going to repeat today. In math we call that multiplication. If I gave you one cookie, how many would you have? One, of course! What if I gave you one cookie two different times? Then how many would you have?

2 cookies

I repeated my action. I gave you a cookie two times. One cookie two times is two cookies. We say one times two equals two.

If I gave you three cookies one time, how many would you have?

three Three times one equals three.

Any number one time equals that same number. If your mom gave you a million kisses one time, how many kisses would she have given you?

a million

How many cookies would you have if I gave you three cookies two times?

six cookies Three plus three is six.

How many cookies would you have if I gave you one cookie seven times?

seven That's one plus one plus one plus one plus one plus one plus one.

B. If your mom asked you to pick up ten things from the floor three times a day, how many things would you pick up in one day?

30 Ten three times is thirty. That's the same as 10 + 10 + 10. Ten times three is thirty.

If your mom asked you to pick up ten things from the floor five times a day, eight times a day or ten times a day, how much would you pick up each time? (Hint: You are counting by tens. Even simpler, you are adding a zero onto the number.) (Note: You could use the hundred chart on Day 7 to help them count by tens.)

50, 80, 100

C.   What if you received six thank you notes nine times? How many would you have received all together?

54 cards   9 x 6 = 54   When you multiply by 9, there are many tricks you can use. The digits in the answer always add up to nine. When learning the facts, you can even use your fingers. If you put down your sixth finger, you'll have 5 and 4 fingers left up, 54.

What about these amounts of cards received nine times? 4, 8, 7, 2

36 cards, 72 cards , 63 cards, 18 cards

D.   Let's keep multiplying by nine. The digits in your answer will add up to a multiple of 9! Let's say you picked 46 things from the yard nine times in a day. How many did you pick up all together?

414 things

What if you picked up 27 things, 51 things, or 246 things? To multiply by hundreds just break it apart.

200 x 9 and 40 x 9 and 6 x 9 is just 2 x 9 with two zeros added to 4 x 9 with one zero added to 6 x 9.

243 things, 459 things (4 + 5 + 9 = 9 + 9 = 18), **2214 things**

Day 17
Problem Solving

We are to forgive our debtors. (Matthew 6:9-15)

A.

-10 -9 -8 -7 -6 -5 -4 -3 -2 -1 0 1 2 3 4 5 6 7 8 9 10

If we have a debt of 1 dollar, how many dollars do we need to get rid of our debt and get to zero dollars? Use the number line. Where would you put your finger to show a debt of one dollar? If you put your finger on 1, you would have one dollar. That's not right. We have minus one dollar. We have one dollar less than nothing! Put your finger on minus one, -1. How many lines do you need to jump to get to zero, to be out of debt?

1 We need one dollar to be out of debt.

If we had two dollars of debt, how many dollars would we need to get out of debt, to get to zero? What if we had five dollars of debt? Ten dollars of debt? (Note: Let them use the number line.)

$2, $5, $10

B.   If you had five dollars of debt, how many dollars do you need to get rid of your debt and have five dollars left over? Use the number line. You are going to begin at minus five and end up at five. How many lines would you need to jump?

10 dollars

How many dollars would you need to get to five dollars if you had two dollars of debt? Four dollars of debt? Ten dollars of debt?

$7, $9, $15

C.   If you had fifteen dollars of debt, how many dollars do you need to get rid of your debt and have twenty-five dollars left over?

40 dollars

How many dollars would you need to get to forty-two dollars if you had sixteen dollars of debt? One hundred forty-eight dollars of debt? Twenty-seven dollars of debt?

$58, $190, $69

D.   If you had one hundred fifty-six dollars of debt, how many dollars do you need to get rid of your debt and have three hundred forty-five dollars left over?

501 dollars

How many dollars would you need to get to three hundred forty-seven dollars if you had two hundred sixty-three dollars of debt? Seventy-nine dollars of debt? Four hundred twenty-eight dollars of debt?

$610, $426, $775

Day 18 (blocks)
Place Value

Don't store up treasures on earth; store up treasures in heaven. (Matthew 6:16-21)

A. Let's divide our treasure to count it more easily. If you had 23 pieces of treasure, you could organize them by putting them into piles of ten and then having a pile of what's left over. How many piles of ten would you have? How many would be left over? You could use blocks to make piles.

There are two piles of ten and three left over.

You can write that in a chart like this. Do you see the number 23 there?

tens	ones
2	3
1	7

Now divide up a treasure of seventeen pieces. Get a pile of seventeen blocks and make piles of ten. How many can you make? How many are left over?

There is one pile of ten and then seven left over.

Write seventeen on the tens and ones chart.

B. You're going to divide 147 pieces of treasure. How many piles of 100 could you make? How many piles of 10? How many ones? Write it on the chart.

1 hundred, 4 tens, 7 ones

hundreds	tens	ones
1	4	7
	3	1
3	1	2

Write thirty-one onto the chart as well as three hundred twelve.

C.   You're going to divide 2548 pieces of treasure. How many piles of 1000 could you make? How many piles of 100 could you make? How many piles of 10? How many ones? Write it on the chart.

2 thousand, 5 hundred, 4 tens, 8 ones

thousand	hundreds	tens	ones
2	5	4	8
		3	0
3	0	0	1

Write thirty onto the chart as well as three thousand one.

D.   You're going to divide 32,018 pieces of treasure. How many piles of ten thousand could you make? How many piles of 1000 could you make? How many piles of 100 could you make? How many piles of 10? How many ones? Write it on the chart.

3 ten thousand, 2 thousand, 0 hundreds, 1 ten, 8 ones

ten thousands	thousands	hundreds	tens	ones
3	2	0	1	8
2	0	4	0	0
7	4	9	0	2

Add twenty thousand four hundred and seventy-four thousand nine hundred two to the chart as well.

Day 19
Expanded Form

You can't add a single hour to your life. (Matthew 6:22-27)

A.   You can't extend your life, certainly not by worrying, so we're going to expand
      something else today. We're going to expand numbers. This is really easy. You'll
      like it.

      On Day 18 we wrote numbers in place value charts. What numbers are written on
      the chart below?

      tens | ones
       2 | 3
       1 | 7

      23 and 17

      2 tens is how much? It's two tens, or ten two times. Count by ten two times.

      20

      What's 5 tens? What's 8 tens? What's 7 tens?

      50, 80, 70

      Now to expand numbers we break them up into tens and ones like this:

           17 is 10 and 7.
           We write 10 + 7.

      Expand 23, 56 and 81 in the same way. Turn them into addition problems that
      separate the tens and ones.

      20 + 3, 50 + 6, 80 + 1

B.   You can expand numbers with hundreds in the same way.

           287 is 200 + 80 + 7 in expanded form, as we call it.

      Expand 517, 628, and 349.

      500 + 10 + 7, 600 + 20 + 8, 300 + 40 + 9

C.   Expand these numbers: 2571, 1080, 9804, and 6736. Write them in expanded form.

2000 + 500 + 70 + 1, 1000 + 80, 9000 + 800 + 4, 6000 + 700 + 30 + 6

What is this number in standard form (just as a normal number)?

5000 + 700 + 20 + 3

5723

D.   Write these numbers in expanded form: 10507 , 26,784 , 58,001.

10,000 + 500 + 7
20,000 + 6000 + 700 + 80 + 4
50,000 + 8000 + 1

What is this number in standard form?

70,000 + 9000 + 800 + 40 + 6

79,846

Day 20
Review

A.   How many cookies would you have if I gave you four cookies two times?

eight cookies

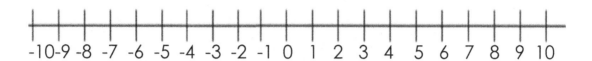

If we had six dollars of debt, how many dollars would we need to get out of debt, to get to zero?

$6

Write 37 and 18 on the chart.

tens	ones
3	7
1	8

What's 6 tens?

60

Expand 74. Turn it into an addition problem that separates the tens and ones.

70 + 4

B. What if your mom asked you to pick up ten things from the floor four times a day? How many things would you pick up in one day?

40

How many dollars would you need to get to six dollars if you had four dollars of debt?

$10

Write it on the chart: two hundred three and seventy-five.

hundreds	tens	ones
2	0	3
	7	5

Expand 729, adding the hundreds, tens, and ones.

700 + 20 + 9

C.   How many cards would you have received if you received nine cards nine times?

81 cards

How many dollars would you need to get to two hundred sixty-three dollars if you had twenty-eight dollars of debt?

$291

Write five thousand three hundred twenty-two on the place value chart.

thousand	hundreds	tens	ones
5	**3**	**2**	**2**

Write seven thousand four hundred thirty in expanded form.

7000 + 400 + 30

What is this number in standard form (just as a normal number)?

2000 + 100 + 90 + 5

2195

D.   What if you picked up 362 things nine times?

3258 things

How many dollars would you need to get to seven hundred forty-nine dollars if you had six hundred eighty-one dollars of debt?

$1430

Write forty seven thousand one hundred fifty-two on the chart.

ten thousands	thousands	hundreds	tens	ones
4	7	1	5	2

Write this number in expanded form: 26,807.

20,000 + 6000 + 800 + 7

Day 21
Adding Tens and Ones

Solomon was clothed in glory. (Matthew 6:28-34)

A.   Solomon probably had lots of royal robes. Let's add them. Think about turning numbers into tens and ones. Below is a chart that shows 23 as two tens and then three ones. Check out the hundred chart on Day 7. Each line is a group of ten numbers. Twenty three is two groups of ten, two lines, and then three ones, three individual blocks. Can you see that on the chart?

Now, you are going to add fourteen to twenty-three. How many tens would you be adding? How many ones? Write fourteen on the chart to show those answers.

```
tens | ones
  2  |  3

  1  |  4
-----+-----
  3  |  7
```

Now add the tens. 2 tens plus 1 ten. What's that? Add straight down and write the answer in the tens' column.

Then add the ones. 3 ones plus 4 ones. Add straight down and find the answer. What is 23 + 14?

37

What if you were to add thirty-five to twenty-three or sixty-one to twenty-three? Write the numbers on the chart and then add the tens and add the ones to find the answers.

```
tens | ones          tens | ones
  2  |  3              2   |  3

  3  |  5              6   |  1
-----+-----          ------+-----
  5  |  8              8   |  4
```

B.   You're going to keep adding tens and ones in a little different way.
      What's 3 + 8? **11** Write that on the tens and ones chart.

```
tens | ones
     |  3
     |
     |  8
  1  |  1
```

What happened? 3 and 8 are ones, but 11 has a ten.
Now we're going to add thirteen and forty-eight. Write them on the chart, but don't add
them yet.

```
tens | ones
  1  |  3
     |
  4  |  8
     |
```

Instead of adding them on the chart, we're going to add the tens and ones
separately and put them together.

So add the tens and ones. 1 ten and 4 tens is 10 + 40. What does that equal?

50

Now add the ones 3 + 8.

11

Now put them together.

```
tens | ones
  5  |  0
     |
  1  |  1
  6  |  1
```

Can you add 15 and 27? Add the tens. Add the ones. Put them together. If it helps you, you could write it on a chart.

42
10 + 20 = 30   5 + 7 = 12

tens	ones	
3	0	30
1	2	+ 12
4	2	42

C.   We're going to add hundreds, tens, and ones. Break them apart and add them together.

174 + 692, 205 + 378, 182 + 208

866, 583, 390
Here's a breakdown of the first one: 100 + 600 + 70 + 90 + 4 + 2 = 700 + 160 + 6

D.   Now you're going to add thousands, tens, and ones. Break them apart and add them together.

4850 + 1367, 2289 + 2298, 3256 + 1749

6217, 4587, 5005
Here's a breakdown of the first one: 4000 + 1000 + 800 + 300 + 50 + 60 + 7 = 5000 + 1100 + 110 + 7 = 6000 + 200 + 10 + 7

Day 22
Symmetry

Don't throw pearls before swine. (Matthew 7:1-6)

A.   We learned today that pearls are symmetrical, two halves are exactly the same shape. Today you are going to practice with symmetry.

Draw one line through each shape to divide it in half. The two halves should be just the same, like it's looking in a mirror.

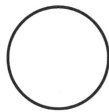  

Down the middle any way in the circle. Down or across the middle of the rectangle. From a point to the middle of the other side on the triangle.

B.   Draw another line on all those shapes to divide them in half another way.

Same answers as above in A. (Note: C will have to find the others.)

C.   Shapes can have multiple, or many, lines of symmetry. How many lines of symmetry does the triangle have? the rectangle? the circle?

3, from each point to the opposite side
2, across the middle, not diagonal – if you folded it in half along that diagonal line the sides wouldn't match up
infinite, there can be a line going through the middle of the circle from any point on the circle to the point on the opposite side

D.   Draw a different shape with four lines of symmetry and one with only one line of symmetry.

A square has four lines of symmetry. A triangle with only two sides the same length has one.

Day 23
Subtracting Tens and Ones

Broad is the path to destruction and narrow the path to life. (Matthew 7:7-14)

A. Let's figure out how much wider is the path to destruction. Let's say the path to destruction was ten feet wide and the narrow path was three feet wide. How much wider is the path to destruction? How would you figure that out? You could draw a picture to help you figure it out. You could draw ten lines. Those could be the ten feet. Then you could circle three of them. Those are the narrow path. What are left over? What's the difference between the large and small paths?

7 feet

How do we get from 10 to 7? We subtract 3. To figure out that problem you needed to subtract. $10 - 3 = 7$ When you need to find the difference between two things, you need to subtract to find it.

You already know how to subtract, so let's subtract with tens and ones today, just like you added. Use the charts below and find the difference between a path of twenty-three feet and one of eleven feet. Then find the difference between a path of 58 feet and 37 feet.

tens	ones
2	3
- 1	1
1	**2**

tens	ones
5	8
- 3	7
2	**1**

B. Let's subtract tens and ones like you added them, by breaking them apart and then putting them back together. 54 is 50 and 4. What is 21? **20 and 1**, What's the difference between fifty-four miles and twenty-one miles? Subtract the pieces. What's 50 minus 20? **30** What's $4 - 1$? **3** What's 30 and 3? **33 and the answer is 33 miles**

Now find the difference between 73 kilometers and 50 kilometers, 64 yards and 32 yards, 48 meters and 27 meters.

23 kilometers, 32 yards, 21 meters

C.   Find the difference between 72 miles and 15 miles, 371 inches and 133 inches, 585 centimeters and 276 centimeters.

57 miles, 238 inches, 309 centimeters

D.   Find the difference between 192 yards and 27 yards, 3984 centimeters and 1790 centimeters, 4872 meters and 2598 meters.

165 yards, 2194 centimeters, 2274 meters

Day 24
Skip counting by ten, Multiplication

Grapes are not gathered from thorn bushes. (Matthew 7:15-23)

A.   Let's gather grapes. First, though, count to 100 by tens, like this: 10, 20, 30, …

Now let's count grapes. Let's say that there are ten grapes on each bunch. Draw five circles and write 10 inside each circle. Touch each one and count grapes like this: 10, 20, … How many grapes are there all together?

50 grapes

How many grapes are on eight bunches of grapes if there are ten grapes on each bunch?

80 grapes

How many grapes are on ten bunches of grapes if each bunch has five grapes?

50 grapes
You can point out how the answer is the same whether you count by ten five times or count by five ten times.

B.   Let's gather more grapes. Let's say we were gathering bunches of grapes that each had 20 grapes on them. How many grapes would be on six bunches? Ten bunches? How many grapes would there be if there were 30 grapes on each bunch and four bunches? Eight bunches?

120 grapes, 200 grapes, 120 grapes, 240 grapes
You are multiplying. To multiply by ten you can just add zero. That changes 1 into 10 and 10 into 100. You know that if you counted by 1 ten times you'd get 10, and that if you count by 10 ten times you'd get 100. That's multiplying by ten. 20 bunches times 10 is 200. For the last qyestion, you can point out to some kids that eight is double four so you just need to double the answer for four bunches.

C. Let's gather more grapes. Let's multiply by 10, 11, and 12. Let's multiply each by 4. Let's break them into parts to multiply.

What are ten, eleven, and twelve in expanded form? **10 and 0, 10 and 1, 10 and 2.**

Now multiply each piece by 4.

10 x 4 = **40**　　　　0 x 4 = **0**　　　　1 x 4 = **4**　　　　2 x 4 = **8**

Now put them together.

10 x 4 = **40 + 0 = 40**　　　11 x 4 = **40 + 4 = 44**　　　12 x 4 = **40 + 8 = 48**

D. Multiply to find the number of grapes. Let's say there 43 bunches of grapes and 12 grapes on each bunch. We can break it apart to multiply. We multiply 43 times 10 and 43 times 2. How many grapes are there all together?

430 and 86 is 516 grapes

How many grapes would there be if there were 52 bunches and 14 grapes on each bunch? (Remember that you can break 52 apart if you need to in order to multiply it by 14.) What about if there were 35 bunches and 15 grapes on each bunch? And what about if there were 83 bunches with 12 grapes on each bunch?

728 grapes, 525 grapes, 996 grapes

Day 25
Review

A.   What if you were to add forty-six to twenty-three or twenty-five to twenty-three? Write the numbers on the chart and then add the tens and add the ones to find the answers.

tens	ones
2	3
4	6
6	9

tens	ones
2	3
2	5
4	8

Draw one line through each shape to divide it in half. The two halves should be just the same, like it's looking in a mirror.

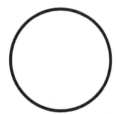  

Down the middle any way in the circle. Down or across the middle of the rectangle. From a point to the other side on the triangle.

Use the chart below and find the difference between a path of 76 feet and 34 feet.

tens	ones
7	6
- 3	4
4	2

How many grapes are on ten bunches of grapes if each bunch has five grapes?

50 grapes

B.   Can you add 14 and 38? Add the tens (10 and 30). Add the ones (4 and 8). Put those answers together to find the final answer.

10 + 30 = 40   4 + 8 = 12   40 + 12 = 52

Draw a shape and two lines of symmetry where each side is a mirror image of the other.

Use the Day 22 lesson if you need help.

Find the difference between 96 yards and 53 yards.

43 yards

How many grapes would there be if there were 20 grapes on each bunch and four bunches?

80 grapes

C.   215 + 179 =

394
Here's a breakdown: 200 + 100 + 10 + 70 + 5 + 9 = 300 + 80 + 14 = 394

How many lines of symmetry does a diamond have? A line of symmetry means that if you folded the shape along that line it would be the same on both sides.

2, across the middle top to bottom and side to side

Find the difference between 72 miles and 15 miles, 371 inches and 133 inches, 585 centimeters and 276 centimeters.

57 miles, 238 inches, 309 centimeters

Multiply 12 by 5. Break it into parts to multiply.

12 x 5 = **50 + 10 = 60**

D.   4961 + 1070 =

6031
Here's a breakdown: 4000 + 1000 + 900 + 60 + 70 + 1 = 5000 + 900 + 130 + 1

How many lines of symmetry does a plus sign have? How about the number 8?

4, 2

Find the difference between 4634 meters and 2452 meters.

2182 meters

How many grapes would there be if there were 34 bunches and 17 grapes on each bunch?

578 grapes
Breakdown: 34 x 10 = 340   34 x 7 = 210 + 28 = 238   340 + 238 = 578

Days 26 - 35

Each workbook level has its own problems. They will be doing vertical math problems. Show them how the problems have the hundreds, tens, and ones lined up to make it easy to add them together. They should always write vertical problems that way with the numbers lined up to make it easy to add the right numbers together.

A.

Day 26
Addition: 17, 13, 10, 11, 13, 14
Ordinals: Jacob
Skip counting: 30
Time: 3:00
Time: AM

Day 27
Addition: 20, 40, 54, 57
Ordinals: Isaac
Skip counting: 18
Time: 1:00
Time: PM

Day 28
Addition: 18, 16, 16, 13, 12, 15
Word problem: 11 miles
Word problem: 14 bushels
Geometry: A circle can be divided in half many ways.

Day 29
Addition: 47, 76, 67, 69
Word problem: 7 miles
Word problem: 7 days
Doubles: 14, 20, 40

Day 30
First Line: 16, 12, 11, 12, 17, 14
Second Line: 30, 50, 56, 67
Third Line: 17, 15, 13, 11, 14, 14
Fourth Line: 48, 67, 47, 58
Fifth Line: 12, 10, 10, 10, 9, 13

A.

Day 31
Subtraction: 8, 7, 5, 7, 8, 7
Word problem: 10 cookies
Word problem: $8

Day 32
Subtraction: 32, 14, 21, 41
Place value: 4|5
Place value: 70
Expanded form: 50 + 7

Day 33
Subtraction: 6, 4, 7, 9, 6, 9
Place value: 17
Place value: 40
Expanded form: 60 + 7

Day 34
Subtraction: 21, 33, 43, 17
Geometry: A triangle is divided in half from a point to the middle of the side across from it. A rectangle is divided in half in the middle from the top to bottom or side to side.
Word problem: 80 grapes

Day 35
First Line: 9, 8, 6, 8, 9, 4
Second Line: 26, 3, 53, 22
Third Line: 7, 5, 8, 6, 8, 8
Fourth Line: 24, 71, 41, 12
Fifth Line: 2, 2, 3, 3, 3, 5

B.

Day 26
Addition: 30, 40, 50, 58, 40, 53
Ordinals: Jacob
Skip Counting: 16, 22
Time: 3:00
Time: PM

Day 27
Addition: 55, 45, 80, 42, 74, 77
Ordinals: Judah
Skip Counting: 15, 40
Time: 6:30
Time: AM

Day 28
Addition: 61, 64, 96, 81, 74, 34
Word Problem: 17 miles
Skip Counting: 100
Time: 1:00

Day 29
Addition: 67, 55, 89, 73, 75, 63
Word Problem: 29 miles
Skip Counting: 200
Time: 2:30

Day 30
First Line: 39, 60, 75, 67, 51, 74
Second Line: 60 56, 71, 53, 75, 76
Third Line: 42, 46, 57, 69, 63, 35
Fourth Line: 63, 55, 91, 54, 60, 82
Fifth Line: 100

B.

Day 31
Subtraction: 8, 14, 0, 12, 11, 10
Word problem: 20 bushels
Double: 160
Word problem: 56 miles

Day 32
Subtraction: 14, 13, 7, 9, 11, 33
Word problem: 5 days
Geometry: It needs to be divided in half with two lines to make four even(ish) pieces.
Double: 64, 50, 200

Day 33
Subtraction: 25, 45, 13, 9, 5, 9
Word problem: 30 things
Word problem: $11
Place value: 3|7|0, |4|6
Expanded form: 500 + 10 + 7

Day 34
Subtraction: 22, 33, 8, 8, 41, 24
Geometry: A box divided into four even pieces would work.
Word problem: 43 yards
Word problem: 90 grapes

Day 35
First Line: 54, 21, 8, 8, 14, 22
Second Line: 14, 25, 13, 7, 6, 8
Third Line: 43, 25, 7, 4, 32, 54
Bottom: 90, 20, 30, 50

C.

Day 26
Addition: 384, 608, 767, 715, 110
Multiply: 2800
Add: 225
Multiply: 24, 15, 18, 24
        42, 49, 81, 64
        30, 21, 32, 72

Day 27
Addition: 558, 454, 803, 185, 585
Word problem: 253 bushels
Multiply: 180, 480, 320, 560

Day 28
Addition: 1994, 6443, 8626, 826, 230
Word problem: 44 oz.
Word problem: 3 days
Double: 150, 98, 300

Day 29
Addition: 5843, 4966, 8692, 733, 716
Word problem: 72 cards
Place value: 1627
Expanded form: 4107
Standard form: 3205

Day 30
Addition: 398, 571, 762, 685, 524
Addition: 605, 570, 716, 543, 532
Multiply: 210, 630, 78, 36, 64
Bottom: 420

C.

Day 31
Subtraction: 15, 183, 484, 274, 72
Addition: 603
Multiply: 51, 144, 57, 75

Day 32
Subtraction: 135, 227, 68, 87, 118
Time: 1:55
Area: 48 blocks

Day 33
Subtraction: 247, 449, 42, 86, 52
Fraction: Draw a shape and divide it in half twice to make four even pieces. Color in three.
Word problem: $412
Multiply: 68, 128

Day 34
Subtraction: 208, 326, 79, 385, 382
Symmetry: 3
Difference: 446 miles
Multiply: 108, 184

Day 35
Subtraction: 462, 309, 76, 78, 78
Subtraction: 432, 191, 767, 336, 72
Subtraction: 60, 90
Multiply: 124, 252
Multiply: 140, 144

D.

Day 26
Addition: 571, 384, 582, 1000
Time: 1:55 (The hour hand keeps moving. It's almost two, so the hour hand is almost at
two.)
Word problem: 960 hours
Word problem: 48 miles

Day 27
Addition: 637, 418, 629, 1000
Time: 10:11
Addition: 898
Word problem: $1030

Day 28
Addition: 631, 437, 644, 521
Place value: 5|6|2|5|9
Expanded form: 40,000 + 3000 + 80 + 5
Word problem: 512 bushels

Day 29
Addition: 723, 821, 613, 714
Add: 1007
Multiply: 37,100
Word problem: 238 cm^2

Day 30
First Line: 8, 9, 8, 8
Second Line: 7, 5, 6, 7
Third Line: 6, 4, 7, 3
Fourth Line: 360, 192, 189, 90
Fifth Line: 536, 104, 351; 31,500
Sixth Line: 810, 1092, 1833, 1596

D.

Day 31
Subtraction: 247, 305, 86, 486
Word problem: 172 grams
Word problem: 8 days
Fractions: three quarters

Day 32
Subtraction: 190, 268, 166, 80
Double: 952
Word problem: 1068 things
Add: 6642

Day 33
Subtraction: 201, 27, 78, 225
Word problem: 2
Word problem: 4256 meters
Word problem: 784

Day 34
Subtraction: 187, 351, 17, 28
Multiply: 19,200
Add: 1205
Word problem: 435 cm^2

Day 35
First Line: 9, 4, 7, 9
Second Line: 4, 6, 7, 5
Third Line: 8, 6, 8, 4
Fourth Line: 270, 296, 168, 356
Fifth Line: 464, 423, 252, 7500
Sixth Line: 476, 2356, 3190, 1363

Day 36
Perimeter (A: making 10)

They want Jesus out of their region. (Matthew 8:28-34)

A. We're going to figure out how big the measure around the region was. That's called the perimeter. To figure out the perimeter we add up the measure all the way around it. Look at the regions below and figure out their perimeters by adding up the measures around their borders. Let's say that all the measurements are in miles. Now for a hint: since there are a lot of numbers to add, add them in a way that makes it easier for you. Look for numbers that you can combine to make ten. Find combos of tens and then add them together first.

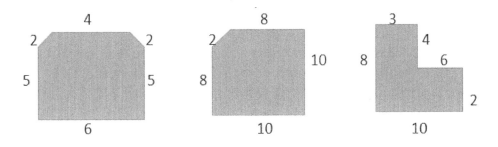

24 miles, 38 miles, 33 miles

B. Find the perimeters of these shapes. Let's say the measurements are all in kilometers. Each kilometer is a little more than half a mile. The shapes all have perimeters that measure more than 100 kilometers. Let's practice one first since you're not used to adding up that high. Let's add the perimeter of a square with a side of twenty-six. You can look at the picture below on the right and think 26 instead of 29. To add you break apart the numbers into tens and ones. What's 26 in tens and ones? **20 + 6** So to add around a square we add those four times. 20 + 20 + 20 + 20 + 6 + 6 + 6 + 6 = 40 + 40 + 12 + 12 ⁻ 80 + 20 + 4 = 100 + 4 = 104 You can break apart and add the numbers however it seems easiest to you.

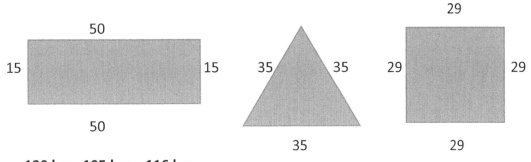

130 km., 105 km., 116 km.

C.   Find the perimeter of these shapes by using multiplication. Let's say all the measurements are yards.

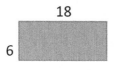

18

6

37

59

48 yd., 148 yd., 295 yd.
6 x 2 = 12 and 18 x 2 = 36
30 + 10 + 2 + 6 = 40 + 8 = 48 You can break apart and add the numbers however it is easiest for you. Just remember that you can always add the tens and ones separately at any time. You're still adding the same amount.
37 x 4 = 30 x 4 and 7 x 4 = 120 + 28 = 148
59 x 5 = 50 x 5 and 9 x 5 = 250 + 45 = 295
When multiplying by a number with a zero on the end, you can just take it off, multiply normally, and then tag it onto the end of the answer. 30 x 4 is 3 x 4 with a zero tagged onto the answer. 12 with a zero tagged on is 120. The same goes for 50 x 5. That's 5 x 5 with a zero tagged onto the answer. 25 with a zero tagged on is 250.

D.   Use multiplication to find the perimeter of these shapes. Let's say all the measurements are in meters.

39

235

16

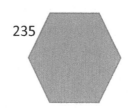

142

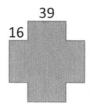

710 m., 1410 m, 284 m
142 x 5 = 100 x 5 and 40 x 5 and 2 x 5 = 500 + 200 + 10 = 710
235 x 6 = 200 x 6 and 30 x 6 and 5 x 6 = 1200 + 180 + 30 = 1410
16 x 8 + 39 x 4 = 80 + 48 + 120 + 36 = 200 + 70 + 14 = 284
When you multiply by a number with a zero on the end, you can just take it off and then tag it back onto the answer. 100 x 5 is 1 x 5 with two zeros tagged onto the answer. 1 x 5 is 5 and 5 with two zeros tagged on is 500.

Day 37 (cubes, square blocks)
Area

They lowered the paralytic down on a bed. (Matthew 9:1-8)

A.   We're going to figure out how big the bed was. We're going to find its area. To do that you might want to get out some blocks, or you can draw some blocks. Let's say the bed was three blocks wide and five blocks long. How many blocks make up the area of the bed? Build it with blocks or draw a picture to find out.

15 blocks

You can also add to find the area. There are three rows of five blocks in each row or five rows with three blocks in each row. No matter how you look at it, there are still fifteen blocks. You can count the rows with five blocks by counting by fives. Count by fives three times. Hold up three fingers and count by fives while you touch each finger.

You just figured that five times three is fifteen. In other words that five three times is fifteen.

What would be the area of the bed if it were four blocks by five blocks or six blocks by five blocks? Count by fives to find the answer.

20 blocks, 30 blocks

B.   You are going to figure out the area of a bed in the same way, but let's say that the bed is 4 blocks across and 10 blocks long. What could you count by to easily add up those blocks? **10** How many times would you need to count by ten? **4** What's the area of the bed?

40 blocks

You multiplied four times ten. Multiplying is just adding over and over again. Counting by tens is just adding ten over and over again.

What would be the area of a bed that was 6 blocks by 10 blocks or 7 blocks by 10 blocks or twenty by ten blocks?

60 blocks, 70 blocks, 200 blocks

C.   When you find the area of a rectangle, like a bed, you are multiplying the length times the width. I'm going to give you measurements instead of blocks. When you multiply inches by inches, you end up with inches squared. We write it like this:

in.^{2}

Let's say each block we measured with was one inch across in each direction. When we are measuring area, we aren't just measuring across a line. One block takes up a whole square. It measures in two directions at once. One block goes one inch along the width and one inch along the length.

Draw a picture of a block and label the length and width each as 1 in. That's a square inch. Right? It's a square that measures an inch. We don't say it measures an inch by an inch. It's an inch squared, an inch in a square shape.

We measure area that way, measuring the width and length together in square measurements. Just picture those blocks filling the bed. Each is a square.

Find the area of these beds: 27 in. by 50 in., 36 centimeters by 80 cm., 4 feet by 7 ft.

1350 in.^{2}, 2880 in.^{2}, 28 ft.^{2} Don't forget the labels!
Here's the first one: 27 x 50 = 20 x 50 and 7 x 50 = 10 (with two zeros tagged on) + 35 (with one zero tagged on) = 1000 + 350 = 1350

D.   How would you find the area of a shape like this, using what you know? (Hint: Turn it into two rectangles.)

8m   12m

16 meters

You would draw a straight line across from the top of the left side. That would make a rectangle on the bottom half. That area would be length times width, or 8 x 16. To find the top half you just notice that it's half a rectangle. If you draw a line straight across from the top point on the right and then a line connecting it with the left side, you would make a skinny rectangle up top. What would be its area? Length, 16, times width, 12-8. Divide that area in half to get the area of the triangle that's actually part of the shape. Add that to the measure of the area of the bottom rectangle. 8 x 16 + (4 x 16)/2 = 128 + 32 = 160 meters squared, 160 m^2 Dividing by two is multiplying by one half, and you can multiply in any order, so you can just take half of sixteen and multiply that by four to make it easier.

Day 38 (two pencils – or pens – three for level D)
Angles

Jesus was reclining at the table. (Matthew 9:9-17)

A.   Thinking of Jesus reclining made me think of angles. How do you think he might have been reclining, or leaning back? If his head were A, where would his feet be?

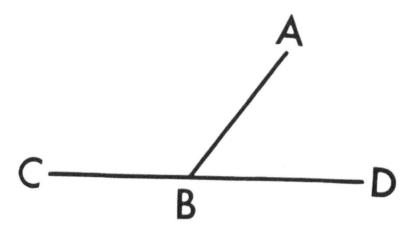

C would be the reclining position.

Today we're talking about angles. Angles are the measure of the space formed where two lines come together. You could also think of it as how far around a circle one line is turned from another.

Maybe it would be easiest to demonstrate for yourself. Take two pencils or pens. Put them on top of each other. There is no space between them. What do you think is the measure of that angle?

0 degrees   We measure angles in degrees.

Try to keep the erasers or tips touching and spin the top pencil all the way around and back to the other. You're drawing a circle shape with your pencil. That measure is 360 degrees. One full circle always measures 360 degrees.

Now you try it. Stand at zero degrees. Now turn 360 degrees. (Spin all the way around.)

Draw 360 degrees on our ABCD picture. Start on the line on the C side and draw a circle that crosses the A line and the D side and goes back to C.

B.   Now what would be the measure of a half circle? If you took those two pencils and turned one to point the opposite way of the other so that they are in a straight line. That would be half a circle, what would be the measure of the angle between them? (Hint: Half the measure of a full circle.)

180 degrees

That would be the measure from where to where on our ABCD picture?

The line C to D.

Lines have the angle measure of $180°$. That's how we write degrees.

Now take your two pencils and turn one halfway to the straight line. What's the measure of the angle going to be?

90°
It's half the way to a straight line, so the angle measure is half of a straight line. 9 + 9 =18 so 90 + 90 = 180

Now you try it. Stand at zero. Turn 360 degrees. (Full circle). Turn 180 degrees (turn and face the opposite direction). Turn 90 degrees (turn to one side or the other).

C.   A tool we use to measure angles is called a protractor. Use the protractor picture included to estimate, guess, what angle you think is made by ABC and ABD. We know that the line CD is how many degrees? **180°** So the angles on either side of the A line added together have to be 180. Make a good guess as to what they might be.

Maybe 120 and 60. You don't have to have that answer to be correct. They just need to add to 180, and one needs to be significantly bigger than the other.

D.   Take three pencils about the same length and make a triangle. Now lower two sides and make them into a straight line. Now put them back into a triangle. How big is the measure of a straight line? **180°** Your triangle is just closing in those measures. The three inner angles made at each point add up to 180. If the sides are all the same length, the angles are the same length. What's the angle?

60°
60 + 60 + 60 = 180 because 6 x 3 = 18.
You can also figure this out 180 divided by 3. That's 18 ÷ 3 with a zero tagged on.

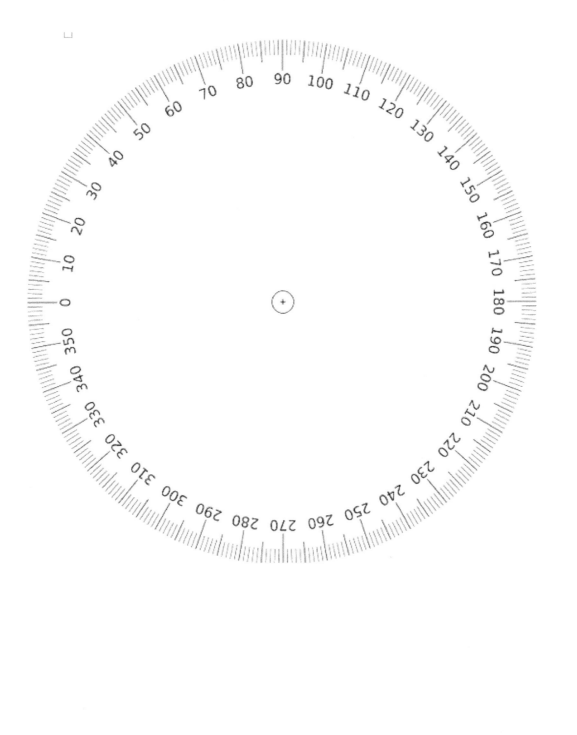

Day 39
Calendar Time D: Long division introduction

The woman had been bleeding for twelve years. (Matthew 9:18-26)

A.   We're going to talk about how long years are today.

          Do you know how many days are in a year?

          365, unless it's what we call a leap year

          A leap year has one extra day. It happens every four years. How many days are in a leap year?

          one more, 366

          How many months are in a year?

          12

          Do you know what they are?

          January, February, March, April, May, June, July, August, September, October, November, December

          Do you know how many days are in a week?

          7

          Do you know the days of the week?

          Sunday, Monday, Tuesday, Wednesday, Thursday, Friday, Saturday

B.   Do you know how many weeks are in a year?

          52

          How many days are in a month?

          28, 29, 30, or 31

          Here's how to tell. Make a fist. Touch the knuckle on your pinky finger and say January. Now touch the in between space, the valley between the knuckles, and say February. Touch the next knuckle and say March. Keep going through July. That's the last knuckle. Jump back to the first knuckle and say August and keep going through December.

Every time you touch a knuckle that month has 31 days. Every time you touch a valley that month has 30 days.

The only exception is February. February only has 28 days. It has 29 days during leap year (any year you can divide by the number four.)

How many days does July, August, September, and October have all together?

123 days
31+31+30+31 = 30 + 30 + 30 + 30 + 1 + 1 + 1 = 60 + 60 + 3 = 6 + 6 (with a zero tagged on) + 3 = 120 + 3
I wouldn't recommend writing out all these steps, just whatever numbers are necessary for them so they don't have to do it all in their head.

C.   How many seconds are in a minute? How many hours are in a day?

60, 24

How many minutes are in a day?

1440 minutes
24 x 60 = 20 x 60 and 4 x 60 = 1200 + 240
24 x 60 = 20 x 6 and 4 x 6 = 120 + 24 = 1440 (with the zero tagged back on)
To multiply numbers with a zero at the end, you can just ignore them and then tag them onto the answer. If there are two zeros in the problem, such as 20 x 60, then there have to be two in the answer.

How many minutes are in a week?

10,080 minutes
1440 x 7 = 144 x 7 with a zero tagged on = 100 x 7 and 40 x 7 and 4 x 7 = 700
+ 280 + 28 = 700 + 200 + 80 + 20 + 8 = 900 + 100 + 8 = 1008 with a zero tagged on

D.   Let's divide by four and see if these years are leap years.

2016 ÷ 4 = 504 Let's see how to figure that out.

When you divide, you can picture a barrel. Let's say that in the barrel are boxes of toys. In each box of toys there are 4 little toys. If there were 92 toys in the barrel, how many boxes were there?

If we take one box out of the barrel, how many toys did we take out of the barrel?

4

If we take ten boxes out of the barrel, how many toys did we take out?

40

If we take one hundred boxes out of the barrel, how many toys did we take out?

400

We don't have that many toys, but I hope you get the idea. We're going to take out toys in batches, groups of hundreds, tens, and ones. Doing that makes the math easier. It's easy to work with the zeros in tens and hundreds.

We can't take out 400 toys. We know that. We only have 92. Can we take out 10 boxes which would be 40 toys? **yes** How many batches, or groups, of ten can we take out?

2
If that's too hard to figure out just take out ten at a time. I'll demonstrate both in just a moment.

If we take out 2 batches of ten, how many boxes did we take out? **20**

If we took out 20 boxes, how many toys did we take out?

80 toys
20 boxes x 4 toys in each box = 80 toys

If we take out 80, how many toys are left in the barrel? How do you find that out?

You subtract what you took out. 92 – 80 = 12 toys

We can't take out another group of 10 boxes. We'll have to take them out one box at a time. How many can we take out? Why?

3, 3 boxes x 4 toys = 12 toys

Groups	Total
	92
20	- 80
	12
3	- 12
23	0

You can write it on a chart like this.

We've taken out 20 boxes with is 80 toys (20 x 4).
There are twelve toys left in the barrel.
We can take out three boxes. 3 x 4 = 12
We took out 23 boxes and there are no toys left in the barrel.

Groups	Total
	92
10	- 40
	52
10	- 40
	12
1	- 4
	8
1	- 4
	4
1	- 4
23	0

Here it is if you aren't sure how many you can take out.

Let's solve $2016 \div 4 = 504$. If we can divide a year by 4 and there are no "years" left in the barrel, then it is a leap year.

Groups	Total
	2016
500	- 2000
	16
4	- 16
504	0

5 x 4 = 20, but I need 2 more zeros to get to 2000, so 2 zeros get tagged onto the 5
4 x 4 = 16

Groups	Total
	874
200	- 800
	74
10	- 40
	34
8	- 32
218	2

Let's do the year 874.
2 x 4 = 8, but I need 2 more zeros to get to 800, so 2 zeros get tagged onto the 2
10 x 4 = 40

8 x 4 = 32 You have to brainstorm what you can multiply by 4 to get to or close to your number or you can just take away eight at a time.

We can't take 4 away again and there are 2 left over, so 874 is not a leap year. Try these all again on your own.

Day 40
Review

A.   Find the perimeter of the shape. Look for numbers that add to ten to make it easy! Let's say that each number represents a meter.

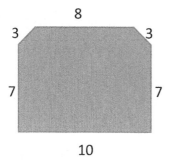

8
3   3
7   7
10

38 meters

Find the area of a bed that three blocks wide and four blocks long.

12 blocks

Turn 360 degrees.

Turn all the way around.

How many months are in a year?

12

Tell someone what they are.

January, February, March, April, May, June, July, August, September, October, November, December

How many days are in a week?

7

Tell someone what they are.

Sunday, Monday, Tuesday, Wednesday, Thursday, Friday, Saturday

B.   Find the perimeters of this shape. Let's say each number represents miles.

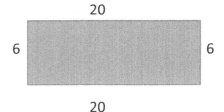

52 miles

Find the area of a bed that's five blocks wide and ten blocks long.

50 blocks

Stand at zero degrees. Turn 360 degrees. Turn 180 degrees. Turn 90 degrees

Full circle, turn and face the opposite direction, turn to one side or the other

How many weeks are in a year?

52

How many days do March, April, May, and June have all together?

122 days
31 + 30 + 31 + 30 = 120 + 2 = 122 days

C.   Find the perimeter of these shapes by using multiplication. Let's say all the measurements are centimeters.

620 centimeters
124 x 5 = 100 x 5 and 20 x 5 and 4 x 5 = 500 + 100 + 20 = 620

Find the area of a rectangle that's 38 inches wide and 70 inches long.

2660 in.² Don't forget the labels!
38 x 70 = 30 x 7 and 8 x 7 = 210 + 56 = 266 (with a zero tagged back on)

On the protractor draw a line from zero to the center. Then draw lines to 50° and 150°.

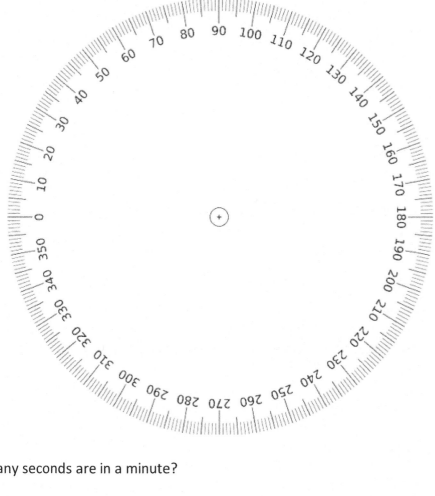

How many seconds are in a minute?

60

How many minutes are in nine hours?

540 minutes
60 x 9 = 540 (just 6 x 9 with a zero tagged on)

How many minutes are in nineteen hours?

1140 minutes
60 x 19 = 10 x 60 and 9 x 60 = 600 + 540 = 1140
You already have the answer to 9 x 60. You just need to add the amount of minutes for ten hours. To multiply by ten you just add zero. 60 becomes 600. The answer is the answer for nine hours plus 600.

D.   Use multiplication to find the perimeter of this shape. Let's say all the measurements are in miles.

317

1902 miles
317 x 6 = 300 x 6 and 10 x 6 and 7 x 6 = 1800 + 60 + 42 = 1000 + 800 + 100 + 2

Find the area of this shape.

6m   8m

17 meters

119 meters
17 x 6 and half of 2 x 17 But half of two is one , so it's just 17 x 6 plus 17 x 1.
10 x 6 and 7 x 6 and 17 = 60 + 42 + 17 = 110 + 9 = 119

A rectangle is just a squashed circle. The four angles formed by its corners add up to 360° just like a circle. How many degrees is each corner?

90°

Use a Groups and Totals chart to show that 360 ÷ 4 = 90 and 513 is not a leap year.

Groups Total   Groups   Total
              360   513
90   - 360   (9 x 4 = 36)   100   - 400   (4 x 100 = 400)
90   0   113
                                                 20   - 80   (4 x 20 = 80)
                                                        33
                                             8   - 32   (4 x 8 = 32)
                                              128   1

It doesn't divide evenly. There's one left over.

Day 41

Word Problems C: extra information D: multi-step

The harvest is plentiful, but the workers are few. (Matthew 9:35-10:4)

A.   Let's figure out how many workers we need for the harvest. Let's say there is enough harvest for ten workers to gather, but there are only three workers. How many more workers are needed? How do you figure that out? What do you need to do? (Note: If they aren't sure, have them draw ten lines for the ten workers needed. Then circle three of them to show which ones we have. The remaining ones are the workers we still need. To get from ten to seven we have to subtract the three.)

7 workers

What if there was enough harvest for 17 workers, but there were only 9 workers? What if there was enough harvest for 36 workers, but there were only 15 workers? What if there was enough harvest for 48 workers, but there were only 23 workers?

8 workers, 21 workers, 25 workers

B.   Let's say there were 7 workers and 4 more were needed in order to bring in the harvest. How many workers were needed for the harvest? What do you need to do to figure this out? (Note: They are going to need to add. If they need a picture, they can draw 7 lines and then draw 4 more on to show how many they would need altogether.)

11 workers

How many workers are needed for the harvest if there are 25 and 36 more are needed? What about if there were 32 workers and 49 more workers are needed? What if there 17 workers and 54 more were needed?

61 workers, 81 workers, 71 workers

C.   Let's say there is enough planted for two hundred fifty-three workers to harvest, but right now there's only enough harvest ready to gather for one hundred fifty-one workers. There are twenty-three workers available at the moment. How many more workers are needed to bring in the harvest right now? What do you need to do to solve this problem? (Hint: If they don't know where to start, read it again with smaller numbers. Using smaller numbers is a great technique for figuring out how to find the answer. They planted enough for twenty, but there's only enough ready for 10 workers. There are 2 workers ready to go, how many more do they need?)

128 workers

253 is an extraneous number. 151 − 23 = 100 and 50 − 20 and 1 − 3 = 30 − 2 = 28

How many workers are needed for the harvest if there is only three hours left until it must come in, and there are four hundred sixty-three workers and one hundred forty-two more needed?

605 workers

463 + 142 = 500 + 100 + 5
The time is extraneous information.

D.   Let's say there's enough harvest for three hundred fifty-nine workers and there are two hundred twenty-eight workers there but thirty-five of them aren't available right now. How many more workers are needed right now to bring in the harvest?

166 workers

228 − 35 = 200 − 10 + 3 = 193 workers available
359 − 193 = 300 − 100 and 50 − 90 and 9 − 3 = 200 − 40 + 6 = 166 workers needed

How many workers are needed for the harvest if there are 625 workers, but 117 aren't available right now, and 280 more are needed.

788 workers are needed for the harvest

625 − 117 = 600 − 100 and 20 − 10 and 5 − 7 = 500 + 10 − 2 = 508 available workers
508 + 280 = 700 and 80 and 8 = 788
Really they could subtract the 117 from 280 if they wanted to or add them together and then subtract it off.

Day 42 (coins, 12 of each type or print them out)
Money

They weren't to take coins in their money belt. (Matthew 10:5-15)

A.   Have your child lay pennies out in three rows of four. Have your child count the value of the coins (one cent, two cents, etc., to twelve cents). Repeat with nickels, counting by fives, and dimes, counting by tens. Lay out the quarters. Practice counting by 25: 25, 50, 75, 100 by counting each row separately. Each row of quarters is how much money?

100 cents which is 1 dollar

How much money is all together in the three rows of quarters?

3 dollars

B   This time lay out a long line of coins like this: three quarters, three dimes, three nickels, three pennies. Have your child start with adding the value of the pennies. Then start with the nickels and keep counting on the pennies. Do it again starting with the dimes. Tell your child it's easiest to start with the largest value. Then finally start with the quarters and count on the rest

$1.23

C.   Grab a handful of coins and have your child count the value. Then give your child this problem. If there are four rows and each individual row has the same kind of coin in it (but the rows can be different from each other), what coins are in the rows if the total value of all of the rows is 66 cents. Let them use the coins to figure it out. **2 rows of dimes, 2 rows of pennies** What if the total value were 90 cents? **2 rows of dimes, 2 rows of nickels** What if the total value were 111 cents? **1 row of quarters, 1 row of dimes, 2 rows of pennies**

D.   (Hint: 10 pennies = 1 dime so 1 penny is one tenth a dime. 5 nickels = 1 quarter so 1 nickel is one fifth of a quarter. 2 nickels = 1 dime so a nickel is half the value) What coins are used if the first and third row have half the value of the second and fourth rows? **nickels, dimes, nickels, dimes** What coins are used if the first row is one tenth of the second row and one fifth of the third row and equal to the fourth row? **pennies, dimes, nickels, pennies** What coins are used if the first row is one fifth of the second row and half of the third row and five times what's in the fourth row? **nickels, quarters, dimes, pennies**

Day 43
Fractions

The apostles were sent out as sheep among wolves. (Matthew 10:16-25)

A.   Let's do sheep and wolf fractions. Draw a square and draw a line to divide it in half. Color in one half. We write fractions like this

$\frac{1}{2}$ or when typing I write them like this ½ or like this $^1/_2$

If there were two animals and one was a sheep and one was a wolf, how could you write as a fraction how many of the animals were sheep? The top number would show how many were sheep. The bottom number would show how many animals there were all together.

½

How would you write the fraction that would show how many were wolves?

½

B.   Write the fraction that would show the number of wolves if there were four sheep and wolves all together and only one was a wolf. Remember that the bottom number shows how many there are all together.

¼

Write the fraction that would show the number of sheep if there were three animals and only one was a sheep?

$^1/_3$

Write the fraction that would show the number of wolves in that scenario?

$^2/_3$
This shows that two out of the three animals were wolves.

C.   The top number in a fraction is called the numerator. What does it show?

how many of the whole group

Let's say that there was a group of eight animals made up of sheep and wolves, and let's say that five were sheep. Write the number of sheep and the number of wolves as fractions. Then use the > greater than sign or the < less than sign to show which fraction is greater (which animal has more). We haven't done this yet this year, but you should recognize these signs. The big end of the sign should point to the bigger number, and the small end of the sign should point to the smaller number.

$^5/_8$ > $^3/_8$
Have them read their answer out loud to you. **five eighths and three eighths**

Do it again with a group of wolves and sheep where there are 13 all together and 7 are wolves.

$^7/_{13}$ > $^6/_{13}$
Have them read their answer to you. **seven thirteenths and six thirteenths**

D.   Draw a horizontal line across the middle of the rectangle. Then draw a vertical line down the middle of the rectangle. Divide each side in half with another vertical line. Divide each of those boxes in half with another vertical line in each one. You should have sixteen boxes, eight on top and eight on bottom. Lightly color in half of the big rectangle. Make sure you can still see all the lines. Write down as many fractions as you can that could be represented by that half. For instance, one half is colored in, but so are two out of the four bigger inside boxes, what else? Those are called equivalent fractions. They are all equal amounts, just written different ways.

$^1/_2$, $^2/_4$, $^4/_8$, $^8/_{16}$

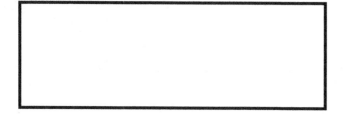

Day 44
Multiplication A: counting above 100 B: counting above 1000

What's told in secret will be proclaimed from the rooftops. (Matthew 10:26-33)

A.   Let's count the number of stairs that we'd need to go up to get to the rooftop. Let's say that there are 13 flights of stairs to get to the roof and that each flight of stairs had ten steps. How many stair steps would you need to climb to get to the top? Let's figure that out. How many steps would you climb to get up one flight? **10** And how many to get up two flights? **20** You just need to count by tens for each flight of stairs. You can use your fingers to help you, or since there are so many flights of stairs, you could write the numbers 1-13 or even just draw 13 lines to represent each flight of stairs. Point to each one as you count by ten. So, how many steps are there to get to the roof?

130 steps

Figure it out now for 17 flights of stairs. What about 20 flights of stairs? (Note: If they are drawing lines, help them to see that they can just add on, not start over. You can try to get them to see that they can just count on from 13 but they may not get that. These are big numbers for them. This is mainly a practice in counting over 100. If they are having fun, you can give them even bigger ones to figure out.)

170 steps, 200 steps

B.   Let's say we have a really huge sky scraper. Let's say there are ten steps in each flight of stairs because that's pretty normal. How many steps would there be every ten floors, every ten flights?

100 steps
You would count by ten, ten times.

Let's say this building has 50 floors in it. How many groups of ten flights of stairs would you have to climb up? (Note: This is how many tens are in fifty.) **5 groups of ten** And how many steps are in the stairs every ten floors? **100 steps** Put them together and figure out how many steps are in a 50-floor building. (Note: This is counting by 100. 100-200-300-400-500)

500 steps

Now figure out how many steps would be in a building with 100 floors, 170 floors, 230 floors!

1000 steps, 1700 steps, 2300 steps

Did they figure out you just need to add a zero onto the number of floors? You can point it out later. Each floor has ten steps. To multiply by ten you are really just adding a zero. (This is mainly an activity to have them using some bigger numbers.)

C.   Let's say that the building has 123 floors and there are 8 steps in each flight of stairs. How would we figure out how many steps there were in all? We multiply the parts. What's 123 in expanded form? **100 and 20 and 3** Multiply 8 by each part. When you multiply by zero, you can just ignore it, multiply normally, and then add it onto the answer of that specific problem. After you multiply each part by 8, add them all together. (You could walk through the first one together if they feel stuck.)

984 steps
100 x 8 and 20 x 8 and 3 x 8 = 800 + 160 + 24 = 984

Now try it with these numbers: 251, 603, 485 each with flights of eight steps each.

2008 steps, 4824 steps, 3880 steps

D.   Let's say that there are 45 flights of stairs and each flight has 12 steps in them. How many stairs are there all together? Again, break it apart to multiply. (Note: You can walk through the first one together at least to get started.)

540 steps
45 is 40 and 5
40 x 12 and 5 x 12 = 40 x 10 and 40 x 2 and 5 x 10 and 5 x 2 = 400 + 80 + 50 + 10

Now let's keep 45 flights of stairs but change the number of steps in each flight. Try it with these numbers: 18, 24, 37.

810 steps, 1080 steps, 1665 steps

Day 45
Review

A.   Let's say there is enough harvest for sixteen workers to gather, but there are only five workers. How many more workers are needed?

11 workers

What if there was enough harvest for 79 workers, but there are only 46 workers?

33 workers

How much money is four quarters?

one dollar

Peter and Andrew were brothers. Peter was also called Simon. Write a fraction that shows how many of the brothers were called two names.

½

Let's say that there are 15 flights of stairs to get to the roof and that each flight of stairs has ten steps. How many stair steps would you need to climb to get to the top?

150 steps

B.   Let's say there were 38 workers and 45 more were needed in order to bring in the harvest. How many workers were needed for the harvest?

83 workers

What about if there were 31 workers and 59 more workers were needed?

90 workers

How much money is three pennies and three nickels?

$0.18

Write the fraction that would show the number of sheep if there were four sheep and wolves all together and only one was a sheep. Remember that the bottom number shows how many there are all together.

¼

Write the fraction that would show the number of wolves in that scenario.

³⁄₄

This shows that three out of the four animals were wolves.

Let's say this building has 750 floors in it. How many groups of ten flights of stairs would you have to climb up?

750 groups of ten

C. Let's say there is enough harvest for one hundred fifty-three workers if it were all ready to come in, but right now there's only enough harvest ready to gather for one hundred twenty-one workers, and there are sixty workers. How many more workers are needed to bring in the harvest right now?

61 workers
153 is an extraneous number.
$121 - 60 = 100$ and $20 - 60$ and $1 - 0 = 100 - 40 + 1 = 61$

What's the value of five nickels, two quarters, six dimes, and seventeen pennies?

$25 + 50 + 60 + 17 =$ 152 cents

Let's say that there was a group of twelve animals made up of sheep and wolves, and let's say that five were sheep. Write the number of sheep and the number of wolves as fractions. Then use the > greater than sign or the < less than sign to show which fraction is greater (which animal has more). (The big end of the sign should point to the bigger number, and the small end of the sign should point to the smaller number.)

⁵⁄₁₂ < ⁷⁄₁₂

Let's say that the building has 812 floors and there are 9 steps in each flight of stairs. How many steps are there all together?

7308 steps
800 x 9 and 10 x 9 and 2 x 9 = 7200 + 90 + 18 = 7308

D. Let's say there's enough harvest for five hundred fifty-nine workers and there are one hundred twenty-eight workers there but seventy-five of them aren't available right now. How many more workers are needed right now to bring in the harvest?

506 workers needed
128 – 75 = 100 – 50 + 3 = 53 workers available
559 – 53 = 500 – 0 and 50 – 50 and 9 – 3 = 500 + 6 = 506

Make up a coin puzzle and give it to an older sibling or a parent to solve.

Write ten equivalent fractions to ½.

Any fraction where the top number is half the bottom number. In other words, any fraction where the denominator is double the numerator.

Let's say that there are 37 flights of stairs and each flight has 24 steps in them. How many stairs are there all together?

888 steps
30 x 24 and 7 x 24 = 30 x 20 and 30 x 4 and 7 x 20 and 7 x 4 = 600 + 120 + 140 + 28

Day 46
Rounding

Jesus spoke to the crowds. (Matthew 11:1-9)

| 10 | 11 | 12 | 13 | 14 | 15 | 16 | 17 | 18 | 19 | 20 |

A. Look at the number line above. If I were to tell you that there were 19 people in the crowd, would you say that was *about* 10 people or 20 people?

19 is much closer to 20 than 10. We call that rounding. We round up or round down to the closest convenient number. If you had to add something to 18, would it be easier to add 19 or 20?

20, of course. It's a nice round number. (Round because it has a nice round 0 on the end.) Sometimes we want an easier number to work with for convenience.

Round these numbers to the nearest ten. That means numbers like 10, 20, 30, 40, 50, 60, ... Which of those is each number closest to?

31 ➔ **30**   58 ➔ **60**   42 ➔ **40**   17 ➔ **20**

B. When a number ends in a 5, it's right in the middle of the number line. We just make the decision to always round it up. So 25 rounds up to 30, 35 rounds up to 40, 45 rounds up to 50, etc.

13 ➔ **10**   35 ➔ **40**   46 ➔ **50**   65 ➔ **70**

| 100 | 110 | 120 | 130 | 140 | 150 | 160 | 170 | 180 | 190 | 200 |

C. We don't have to just round to the nearest ten. We can round to the nearest hundred. Is 125 closer to 100 or 200? It's closer to 100. Is 380 closer to 300 or 400? It's closer to 400. What about 230? What does it round to? **200**

The middle number is 50 this time. 350 rounds up to 400. 450 rounds up to 500. 550 rounds up to 600. Round the numbers below to the nearest hundred.

143 ➔ **100**   450 ➔ **500**   129 ➔ **100**   680 ➔ **700**

D. Round these numbers to the closest hundred.
264 ➔ **300**   949 ➔ **900**   150 ➔ **200**   618 ➔ **600**

Day 47
Estimation

Jesus sent a messenger before Him. (Matthew 1:1-7)

A.   On Day 46 we rounded numbers. Today we're going to estimate, or make a good
      guess, by doing our math with rounded numbers.

      Here's an example. Let's say the messenger went 18 miles and then went 11 miles
      more. About how far did he travel? The word about tells us we don't need an exact
      answer. We can estimate. Let's round to the nearest ten and then add the rounded
      numbers together to get our estimation.

      What does 18 round to? **20**   What does 11 round to? **10**

      Together about how many miles did he travel? **20 + 10 = 30 miles**

      Now figure out exactly how many miles he traveled. 18 + 11 = **29 miles**
      Was your estimated answer a good guess? **Yes!**

      Now try it with these numbers: 27 and 22, 41 and 38, 13 and 66 (all miles). Just
      find the estimates.

      30 + 20 = 50 miles, 40 + 40 = 80 miles, 10 + 70 = 80 miles

B.   Let's say a messenger traveled 78 kilometers and 63 km. KM is the abbreviation
      for kilometers, the short way of writing it. About how far did she travel all
      together? Estimate. Round each number and then add them together.

      80 + 60 = 140 (8 + 6 = 14)

      Now try with these numbers: 44 km and 75 km, 15 km and 57 km, 39 km and 26
      km.

      40 + 80 = 120, 20 + 60 = 80, 40 + 30 = 70 kilometers

C.   Let's say the messenger went 159 miles in one day and 76 of the miles were
      traveled after lunch. About how far did he travel before lunch?

      160 − 80 = 80 miles (16 − 8 = 8)

Now try with these numbers: 170 and 29, 114 and 68, 155 and 82.

170 − 30 = 140 miles, 110 − 70 = 40 miles, 160 − 80 = 80 miles

D. Let's say that the messenger traveled 120 minutes before breakfast, 254 minutes after breakfast and before lunch, and another 531 minutes before sleeping. About how many hours did he travel that day? What are you going to need to do to solve this problem? **Add up the rounded number of minutes and then divide by 60.** (Note: They can round to the nearest ten or hundred.)

Groups	Total	
	900	
10	− 60	(10 x 6 = 60)
	30	
5	− 30	(5 x 6 = 30)
15	0	

100 + 300 + 500 = 900
120 + 250 + 530 = 900

How to divide by 60? 60 is 6 x 10.
You can divide by 6 and divide by 10,
just like you would break up other numbers.
To multiply by 10, what trick can you use?
Just add a zero.
To divide by 10, you can do the opposite.
Take off a zero.

Divide 900 by 60 by dividing by ten (taking off a zero) and then dividing by six.

15 hours

Now try with these numbers by rounding to the nearest hundred: 204 minutes and 423 minutes, and 720 minutes and 756 minutes.

10 hours (200 + 400 = 600, 600 ÷ 60 = 60 ÷ 6 = 10)
25 hours (700 + 800 = 1500, 1500 ÷ 60 = 150 ÷ 6 = 25)

Day 48
Estimation

Jesus did most of His miracles in their cities. (Matthew 11:20-30)

A.   Let's estimate again today. Let's estimate the total number of miracles. Let's say Jesus did 92 miracles one day in two cities. In the first city He did 37 miracles. About how many miracles did He do in the second city? The word about means to estimate.

First, round the numbers. Then what? (Note: If they don't know what to do, start with little numbers. If He did 5 miracles all day and in the first city He did 3, how many did He do in the second city? They will likely come up with the answer without consciously thinking about subtraction. When they say the answer, ask how they used five and three to get two? They will need to subtract.)

90 – 40 = 50 miracles

Now try with these numbers: 89 miracles all day and 27 miracles in the first city, 71 and 58, 92 and 64.

90 – 30 = 60 miracles, 70 – 60 = 10 miracles, 90 – 60 = 30 miracles

B.   What if Jesus did 99 miracles in one day and 17 miracles in the second city? About how many miracles did He do in the first city? Round the numbers and then answer the question.

100 – 20 = 80   10|0   To subtract 20 from 100, you can subtract the ones
                          _2|0_ and see that what's left is 10 – 2.
                           8|0

Try these numbers: 102 and 45, 75 and 40, 36 and 14.

100 – 50 = 50 miracles, 80 – 40 = 40 miracles, 40 – 10 = 30 miracles

C.   What if Jesus did 289 miracles in each of 8 cities? How many miracles did He do all together? What do you need to do to solve that? **multiply**

Do it three ways. First, estimate by rounding the number of miracles to the nearest 100 and multiply by 8. Then estimate by rounding both the number of miracles and the number of cities to the nearest ten and multiply to find the answer. Then solve the exact answer. (Hint: 341 to the nearest ten is 340.)

300 x 8 = 8 x 3 (and tag on two zeros) = 2400 miracles
290 x 10 = 29 x 1 (with two zeros tagged on) = 2900 or just tag a zero on 290
289 x 8 = 2312 miracles
200 x 8 and 80 x 8 and 9 x 8 = 1600 + 640 + 72 = 1000 + 1200 + 110 + 2

D.   What if Jesus had done 276 miracles in 4 cities? How many miracles did He do in each city? Estimate the answer by rounding to the nearest hundred, then rounding to the nearest ten, and then find the exact answer.

300 ÷ 4 = 75
280 ÷ 4 = 70
276 ÷ 4 = 69

Groups	Total
	300
10	40 (10 x 4)
	260
60	240 (60 x 4)
	20
5	20
75	0

Groups	Total
	280
70	280
70	0

Groups	Total
	276
60	240
	36
8	32
	4
1	4
69	0

I did these a little different. I didn't always pick the highest possible number of groups. Sometimes you don't think of the highest number. That's okay; the multiplication and subtraction is easy because there are lots of zeros.

Day 49
Comparing Numbers

Jesus and His disciples were walking through grainfields. (Matthew 12:1-8)

A. Today we're going to decide which grainfields are the biggest. Let's start with easy numbers. Let's say the field of wheat is seven acres and the field of barley is twelve acres, which one is bigger?

The barley field is bigger, of course. This is how we would show that on paper.

12 > 7   or   7 < 12

That symbol between the numbers is called the greater than/less than sign. It shows which number is bigger. Look carefully and make observations. How does the sign show which number is bigger and which number is smaller?

The big, open end points to the bigger number, and the small, pointy end points to the smaller number.

Put the symbol between the numbers below to show which is smaller and which is bigger.

23 < 51   102 > 78   124 < 160

B. Write which crop is the biggest. The wheat is on ten fields that are 17 acres each. The barley is on three fields that are 58 acres each. Find the total number of acres of each crop and write them next to each other with a greater than/less than symbol.

Wheat field: 170 acres (To multiply by ten you just need to add a zero.)

Barley field: 174 acres
58 + 58 + 58 = 50 + 50 + 50 + 8 + 8 + 8 = 100 + 50 + 16 + 8 = 150 + 10 + 14 = 174
This isn't done in the most efficient way. I'm just showing how you can break down the numbers. Do it however it's easiest for you to think about them.

170 acres < 174 acres

Now try with these numbers.

1897 < 3012   Ten fields of 23 acres   145 + 87

230 < 232

100 + 40 + 80 + 5 + 7 =

100 + 120 + 12 =

100 + 100 + 20 + 10 + 2 =

Again, this isn't the most efficient way. Maybe it's simple for you to just combine in your head 120 and 12. This just shows how you can break numbers apart to make them easier to add.

C. If a wheat field had 7 rows of 72 plants and the barley field had 8 rows of 59 plants, which has more crops? Compare their number of crops using a greater than/less than symbol.

Wheat field: 7 x 72 = 7 x 70 and 7 x 2 = 490 + 14 = 400 + 100 + 4 = 504 plants
Remember that 7 x 70 is just 7 x 7 with a zero tagged on.

Barley field: 8 x 59 = 8 x 50 and 8 x 9 = 400 + 72 = 472 plants

504 plants > 472 plants

Now try it with these numbers:

21,451 > 20,989   9 rows of 462 plants   5 rows of 871 plants

4158 plants < 4355 plants

Walkthroughs:

9 x 462 = 9 x 400 and 9 x 60 and 9 x 2 = 3600 + 540 + 18 = 3000 + 1100 + 50 + 8

5 x 871 = 5 x 800 and 5 x 70 and 5 x 1 = 4000 + 350 + 5

Remember that 5 x 800 = 5 x 8 with two zeros tagged on.

D. If a wheat field had 27 rows of 72 plants and the barley field had 34 rows of 58 plants, which has more crops? Compare their number of crops using a greater than/less than symbol.

Wheat field: 27 x 72 = 20 x 72 and 7 x 72 =

20 x 70 and 20 x 2 and 7 x 70 and 7 x 2 =

1400 + 40 + 490 + 14 = 1000 + 800 + 140 + 4 = 1944 plants

Remember that 20 x 70 is just 2 x 7 with two zeros tagged on.

Barley field: 34 x 58 = 30 x 58 and 4 x 58 =
                  30 x 50 and 30 x 8 and 4 x 50 and 4 x 8 =
                  1500 + 240 + 200 + 32 = 1000 + 900 + 70 + 2 = 1972 plants

1944 plants < 1972 plants

Now let's say there are two fields that are the same size. Half of one field is wheat. Nine sixteenths of the other field is barley. Write them as fractions and show which is bigger? (Hint: What's an equivalent fraction of one half that has sixteen as its denominator?)

$^1/_2 < \, ^9/_{16}$

$^1/_2 = \, ^8/_{16}$ (You can see this on Day 43.)

$8 < 9$ so $^8/_{16} < \, ^9/_{16}$

One quarter ($^1/_4$) of the one field is wheat. Two eighths of the other field is barley. Is the amount of wheat greater than, less than, or equal to the amount of barley? Show why.

$^1/_4 = \, ^2/_8$

To show this you could draw a box and divide it in half both ways to make it into quarters and then color in one quarter, one of the four corners. Then you could draw two more lines to divide it into eight boxes. Two of the eight boxes are in the colored-in section.

Day 50
Review

A.   Round these numbers to the nearest ten. That means numbers like 10, 20, 30, 40, 50, 60, … Which of those is each number closest to?

51 → **50**   38 → **40**   72 → **70**   87 → **90**

Let's say the messenger went 27 miles and then went 41 miles more. <u>About</u> how far did he travel? Round each number and then add them together.

30 miles + 40 miles = 70 miles

Let's say Jesus did 86 miracles one day in two cities. In the first city He did 35 miracles. About how many miracles did He do in the second city?

90 – 40 = 50 miracles

Put a greater than/less than symbol between the numbers to show which is greater and which number is smaller.

42 > 37   100 < 500

B. Round the numbers to the closest ten.

24 → **20**   38 → **40**   45 → **50**   26 → **30**

Let's say a messenger traveled 78 kilometers and 63 km. <u>About</u> how far did she travel all together? Round each number and then add them together.

80 + 60 = 140 (8 + 6 = 14)

What if Jesus did 98 miracles in one day and 26 miracles in the second city? <u>About</u> how many miracles did He do in the first city? Round the numbers and then answer the question.

100 − 30 = 70   10|0   To subtract 30 from 100, you can subtract the ones
                          3|0   and see that what's left is 10 − 3.
                          7|0

Use greater than and less than symbols to compare these numbers.

2897 < 3015   Ten fields of 13 acres   45 + 87
                             130 < 132
                             40 + 80 + 5 + 7 =
                             120 + 12 =
                             100 + 20 + 10 + 2 =

C.   Round these numbers to the nearest hundred.

149 → **100**   650 → **700**   219 → **200**   451 → **500**

Let's say the messenger went 279 miles in one day and 186 of the miles were traveled after lunch. <u>About</u> how far did he travel before lunch? You can round to the nearest hundred.

300 – 200 = 100 miles

What if Jesus did 419 miracles in each of 6 cities? How many miracles did He do all together?

Do it three ways. First, estimate by rounding the number of miracles to the nearest hundred and multiply by 6. Then estimate by rounding both the number of miracles and the number of cities to the nearest ten and multiply to find the answer. Then solve the exact answer. Which was the best estimate?

400 x 6 = 4 x 6 (and tag on two zeros) = <u>2400 miracles</u>
420 x 10 = 42 x 1 (with two zeros tagged on) = 4200 or just tag a zero on 420
419 x 6 = 2514 miracles
400 x 6 and 10 x 6 and 9 x 6 = 2400 + 60 + 54 = 2000 + 400 + 114

Compare these numbers using a greater than/less than symbol.

24,001 > 22,975   8 rows of 247 plants   5 rows of 331 plants
                                      1976 plants > 1655 plants
Walkthroughs:
8 x 247 = 8 x 200 and 8 x 40 and 8 x 7 = 1600 + 320 + 56 = 1000 + 900 + 70 + 6
5 x 331 = 5 x 300 and 5 x 30 and 5 x 1 = 1500 + 150 + 5 = 1000 + 600 + 50 + 5
Remember that 8 x 200 = 2 x 8 with two zeros tagged on.

D. Round these numbers to the closest hundred.

324 → **300** 749 → **700** 650 → **700** 378 → **400**

Let's say that the messenger traveled 200 minutes before breakfast, 364 minutes after breakfast and before lunch, and another 276 minutes before sleeping. <u>About</u> how many hours did he travel that day? Estimate the answer by rounding to the nearest hundred, then rounding to the nearest ten, and then find the exact answer.

900 ÷ 60 = 15 (900 ÷ 60 = 90 ÷ 6)
840 ÷ 60 = 14 (840 ÷ 60 = 84 ÷ 6)
840 ÷ 60 = 14 hours

Groups	Total
	90
10	60 (10 x 6)
	30
5	30 (5 x 6)
15	0

Groups	Total
	84
10	60
	24
4	24
14	0

Groups	Total
	840
10	600
	240
4	240
14	0

What if Jesus had done 184 miracles in 4 cities? How many miracles did He do in each city? Estimate the answer by rounding to the nearest hundred, then rounding to the nearest ten, and then find the exact answer.

200 ÷ 4 = 50
180 ÷ 4 = 45
184 ÷ 4 = 46

Groups	Total
	200
50	200 (5 x 4)
50	0

Groups	Total
	180
40	160 (4 x 4 = 16)
	20
5	20 (5 x 4 = 20)
45	0

Groups	Total
	184
40	160
	24
6	24
46	0

If a wheat field had 37 rows of 73 plants and the barley field had 46 rows of 59 plants, which has more crops? Compare their number of crops using a greater than/less than symbol.

37 x 73 = 30 x 73 and 7 x 73 = 30 x 70 and 30 x 3 and 7 x 70 and 7 x 3 = 2100 + 90 + 490 + 21 = 2000 + 500 + 200 + 1 = 2701 plants
Remember that 30 x 70 is just 3 x 7 with two zeros tagged on.

46 x 59 = 40 x 59 and 6 x 59 = 40 x 50 and 40 x 9 and 6 x 50 and 6 x 9 = 2000 + 360 + 300 + 54 = 2000 + 600 +110 + 4 = 2714 plants

2701 plants < 2714 plants

Day 51
Elapsed Time

Many followed Him. (Matthew 12:15-24)

A.   Let's say a crowd gathered around to listen to Jesus talk at 10 AM. They stayed until noon. How long were they there listening to Jesus? You need to know that noon is 12 PM, right when it turns from AM to PM. It's about lunch time. Draw each time on the clocks below and then write how much time has elapsed, how much time has gone by.

Elapsed time: **2 hours**   Elapsed time: **4 hours**   Elapsed time: **6 hours**

Now try with these times. Noon until 4 PM, 4 PM until 10 PM – For these, just draw the new time. You can use the previous clock to help you count the hours.

B.   Let's say that the crowd followed Jesus as He walked out of the city. Let's say the walk took half an hour. Then they stayed and listened for another two hours. How long did they stay with Jesus?

two and a half hours

If they started walking at 10:00 in the morning, when did they arrive where they were going? Draw the time.

10:30 (AM won't show on the clock)

If they followed Jesus from ten in the morning until three in the afternoon, how long were they with Jesus?

5 hours

Draw these times on the clocks and then write how much time passed from the first to the second. 6:30 and 11:00

Elapsed time: **4 and ½ hours**

C.   Let's say Jesus' followers arrived at 7:35 and stayed until 10:55. How long were they with Jesus? Draw the times and then figure out the elapsed time.

Elapsed time: **3 hours and 20 minutes**   Elapsed time: **15 minutes**

Try again with these times. 11:50 and 12:05, 10:30 and 1:25, 4:15 and 9:40.
To figure out something like 10:30 to 1:25, count on hours from 10:30. 10:30, 11:30, 12:30, 1:30. Then you can take off five minutes. Or, you can stop at two hours and then count on minutes until you reach fifty-five. I think it's easier to go backwards.

Elapsed time: **2 hours and 55 minutes**   Elapsed time: **5 hours and 25 minutes**

D. Let's say Jesus' followers were with Him from 8:02 in the morning until 12:40 in the afternoon. How long were they with Jesus?

4 hours and 38 minutes

Try it with these times: 7:46 AM and 11:07 PM, 10:15 PM to 5:47 AM, midnight to noon

15 hours and 21 minutes, 7 hours and 32 minutes, 12 hours

Day 52
Negative

A house divided against itself cannot stand. (Matthew 10:16-25)

A.

-10 -9 -8 -7 -6 -5 -4 -3 -2 -1 0 1 2 3 4 5 6 7 8 9 10

Do you know your right from your left? Look at the number line. Which numbers are on the right-hand side, positive or negative? **positive** Which numbers are on the left-hand side, positive or negative? **negative**

If we want to get more and more and more, would we need to move on the number line to the right or to the left? **right**

If you wanted less and less and less, would you move to the right or to the left on the number line above? **left**

I want you to put your finger on zero and follow the directions and add each of these numbers by moving your finger that many to the right or to the left. Then write down which number you finish on.

6, - 2, 5, - 10, 1

0
Their finger should have jumped to 6, 4, 9, -1, 0 as they counted up six, down two, up five, down ten and up one.

B.   Add the positive numbers and subtract off the negative numbers to show that 6 and -2 and 5 and -10 and 1 all together make 0. Combine the positive numbers. Combine the negative numbers. You'll see that writing a negative number is just like writing a subtraction sign. Combing 2 and -1 is just $2 - 1 = 1$

$6 + 5 + 1 = 12$
- 2 and - 10 = - 12
Twelve and negative twelve or $12 - 12 = 0$

Combine these numbers. 8, 3, 9, 7, 15, - 20, - 6, - 10, - 1

5
8 + 3 + 9 + 7 + 15 = 11 + 16 + 15 = 30 + 12 = 42
- 20 and - 6 and - 10 and - 1 is - 37 (just add them together)
42 – 37 = 5

C.   The house is completely divided. Half are negative. Half are positive. If there are
       -45, - 120, and – 78, then how many are on the positive side?

243
45 + 120 + 78 = 100 + 110 + 20 + 13 = 243

Combine these numbers. 137, - 63, 82, - 112, 56, - 27

73

D.   Combine these numbers. 1293, - 831, 329, - 718, 650, - 185

538

Divide the "house" in half. What's 315 divided in half? Is there anything left over?
If so, how much? Can you know before you start if there will be anything left over?

157 R1, means remainder 1, one left over
We have found leftovers before, but this is the first time I've written the word
remainder. You can share that word with your child and show how to write it with
an R.

Groups	Total
	315
150	300 (150 x 2 = 300)
	15
7	14
157	1

Day 53
Using zeros

Jonah was in the belly for three days and three nights, and the good tree produces good fruit, and we have to make an accounting. (Matthew 12:33-42)

A.   We're going to do math with zeros today; we'll do our accounting with zeros. Doing math with zeros is fun because it's so easy. Zero plus zero equals? **zero** Zero minus zero equals? **zero** Zero times zero equals? **zero** Just like how a good tree produces good fruit. Zeros make zeros. We'll double numbers since Jonah spent three days and three nights in the deep.

What's double 1? 1 + 1 = **2**
What's double 10? 10 + 10 = **20**
What's double 100? 100 + 100 = **200**
What's double 1000 (one thousand)? 1000 + 1000 = **2000**
What do you think is double one million? **two million**
The number of zeros stays the same after you add or subtract the other numbers.

Double these numbers: 4, 40, 400; 6, 60, 600; 8, 80, 800

8, 80, 800; 12, 120, 1200; 16, 160, 1600

B.   Maybe there is some bad fruit and we need to take it away. Let's say there are 140 pieces of fruit and 70 pieces are bad. How many good ones are left? What do you need to do to figure this out? If you ever aren't sure how to solve a problem, make it simpler. What if there were 14 pieces of fruit and 7 were bad? Then how many were good? **7** How do you get 7 from 14 and 7? **You subtract.**

140 – 70 = 70 pieces of good fruit
To solve this you need to subtract 14 – 7. Then zero minus zero just is the zero on the end.

Try it with these numbers: 90 – 40, 160 – 70, 140 – 80, 800 + 900, 1100 – 300

50, 90, 60, 1700, 800
1100 – 300 is just 11 – 3 with two zeros. You can do it orally and say 11 hundred – 3 hundred is 8 hundred, just like you would say 11 apples – 3 apples is 8 apples.

Read your answers out loud.

C.	When you multiply by zero, it's important to maintain the number of zeros in the original question. 300 times 50 = 3 x 5 with three zeros = 15,000 The trickiest part is when the part you multiply has an answer with zero; make sure you still tag on all the original zeros from the question.

Try this. How many pieces of fruit are in an orchard if there are 80 trees and each tree has 50 pieces of fruit?

4000 pieces of fruit
80 x 50 = 8 x 5 with two zeros = 40 with two zeros = 4000

Now try with these numbers. 400 x 80, 700 x 900, 120 x 400, 500 x 60

32,000; 630,000; 48,000; 30,000

Read your answers out loud.

D.	Division is the opposite of multiplication. So what happens to the zeros? They get taken away instead of added.

Divide one million by ten six times. What's the answer the last time?

1,000,000 ÷ 10 = 100,000
100,000 ÷ 10 = 10,000
10,000 ÷ 10 = 1,000
1,000 ÷ 10 = 100
100 ÷ 10 = 10
10 ÷ 10 = 1

How many zeros were you dividing with? **There is just one zero in ten.** How many zeros disappeared from the answer each time you divided by ten? **one**

Multiplying 8 x 20 is the same as multiplying 8 x 2 x 10. We're allowed to mix and match the numbers as we please. So instead of multiplying 2 x 10 and getting 20 again. We can multiply the 8 x 2 and get something simpler. That's 16 x 10. To multiply by ten, we just add a zero, 160.

Division is the opposite. You can divide 160 by 20 by dividing it by ten and then dividing it by 2. To divide by ten we do the opposite. We take away a zero. 160 divided by 10 is 16. Then we just divide 16 by 2 and get 8.

Break apart these numbers like this 20 = 2 x 10. 40, 90, 500 **4 x 10, 9 x 10, 5 x 100**

Try it with these numbers. 320 ÷ 40, 630 ÷ 90, 1000 ÷ 100, 2000 ÷ 500 **8, 7, 10, 4**

Day 54
Algebra – Missing Numbers

"For whoever does the will of My Father who is in heaven, he is My brother and sister and mother." (Matthew 12:43-50)

A.   Let's figure something out. It's kind of weird to talk about more than one mother, so let's find out the number of brothers and sisters. Let's say Jesus is looking at a group of believers whom He considers His brothers and sisters. And let's say we know the number of believers is twelve and the number of men, the number of "brothers" is five. How would you find the number of sisters?

$$5 + \underline{7} = 12$$

They can think five plus what equals twelve. Or they can think $12 - 5 = 7$.

Now figure out what goes in these blanks.

$$8 + \underline{6} = 14 \qquad\qquad 8 + \underline{9} = 17$$

$$10 + \underline{5} = 15 \qquad\qquad 20 + \underline{20} = 40$$

B.   Find what number fits in these blanks.

$$52 + \underline{23} = 75 \qquad\qquad 45 + \underline{15} = 60$$

$$14 + \underline{8} = 22 \qquad\qquad \underline{35} - 5 = 30 \text{Pay attention!}$$

C.   Find what number fits in these blanks.

$$\underline{93} - 23 = 70 \qquad\qquad 5 \times \underline{15} = 75$$

$$385 + \underline{7} = 392 \qquad\qquad 154 + \underline{67} = 221$$

D. Find what number fits in these blanks. You subtracted to fill in the blank on an addition problem. You added to fill in the blank on an addition problem. What will you need to do to fill in the blank on a multiplication problem? **divide** A division problem? **multiply**

$\underline{6}$ x 23 = 138   5 x $\underline{35}$ = 175

$\underline{5096}$ ÷ 7 = 728 $\underline{2560}$ ÷ 8 = 320

Day 55
Review

A.   Let's say a crowd gathered around to listen to Jesus talk at 6 AM. They stayed until
       noon. How long were they there listening to Jesus? Draw each time on the clocks
       below and then write how much time has elapsed, how much time has gone by.

Elapsed time: **6 hours**

-10 -9 -8 -7 -6 -5 -4 -3 -2 -1 0 1 2 3 4 5 6 7 8 9 10

I want you to put your finger on zero and follow the directions and add each of
these numbers by moving your finger that many to the right or to the left. Then
write down which number you finish on.

4, - 3, 6, - 10, 5

2

Double these numbers: 5, 50, 500

10, 100, 1000

Fill in the missing numbers.

9 + _9_ = 18   7 + _7_ = 14

10 + _20_ = 30   4 + _6_ = 10

B.   If the crowd started walking at 9:00 in the morning, when did they arrive where they were going if they walked for one hour and a half? Draw 9:00 and the time they arrive. Then answer how much time elapsed.

10:30 (AM won't show on the clock)

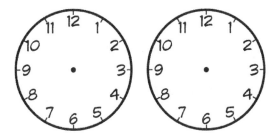

Elapsed time: **1 and ½ hours**

Combine these numbers. 8, 13, 25, 8, - 12, - 10, - 1

31
8 + 13 + 25 + 8 = 54
- 12 and - 10 and - 1 is - 23
54 – 23 = 31

Let's say there are 160 pieces of fruit and 80 pieces are bad. How many good ones are left?

Try it with these numbers: 1200 – 400

80, 800

Find what number fits in these blanks.

43 + _25_ = 68   32 + _27_ = 59

C. Let's say Jesus' followers arrived at 10:25 in the morning and stayed until 1:05 in the afternoon. How long were they with Jesus? Draw the times and then figure out the elapsed time.

Elapsed time: **2 hours and 40 minutes**

Combine these numbers. 153, - 45, 72, - 102, 87, - 19

146

How many pieces of fruit are in an orchard if there are 700 trees and each tree has 60 pieces of fruit?

42,000 pieces of fruit

Find what number fits in these blanks.

_157_ - 57 = 100   278 + _134_ = 412

D. Let's say Jesus' followers were with Him from 6:42 in the morning until 2:30 in the afternoon. How long were they with Jesus? Draw the times and find the elapsed time.

Elapsed time: **7 hours and 48 minutes**

Combine these numbers. 263, - 331, 516, - 418, 240, - 107

163

Divide the "house" in half. What's 527 divided in half? Is there anything left over? If so, how much? Can you know before you start if there will be anything left over?

263 R1, means remainder 1, one left over because it is odd

Groups	Total
	527
250	500 (250 x 2 = 500)
	27
13	26
263	**1**

Divide three hundred thousand by ten.
30,000

$4000 \div 80 =$ **50**

Find the missing number.

<u>8</u> x 34 = 272   <u>580</u> ÷ 4 = 145

Day 56 (coins)
Coin Values

To those who have more will be given in abundance. (Matthew 13:10-17)

A.   We're learning about economics this week, so let's do some money. Let's count coin values. That means you are going to count how much they are worth.

Count coins today.

A penny is worth one cent.

We write $0.01 or 1¢.

A nickel is worth five cents.

We write $0.05 or 5¢.

A dime is worth ten cents.

We write $0.10 or 10¢.

A quarter is worth twenty-five cents.

We write $0.25 or 25¢.

Use your own coins or use cut out coins (print from our site) to pay for the items. (Note: You might want to quiz the coins first and make sure they know their names and values.)

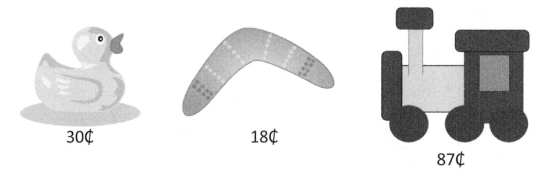

30¢   18¢

87¢

B. Use your coins to buy the items. How many ways can you pay for each item?

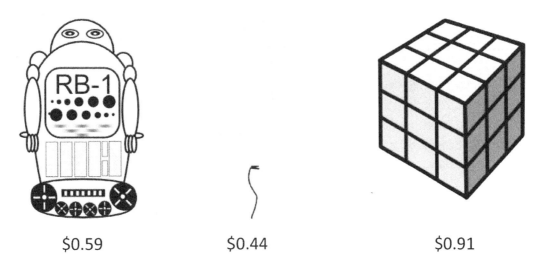

$0.59 $0.44 $0.91

C. How many ways can you make one dollar with coins? Remember that one dollar
is one hundred cents. Use P for Penny, N for Nickel, D for Dime, and Q for Quarter
to write the different combinations. (You can write things like 100 P, but don't use
my example!) Write down at least ten different ways.

Add these amounts together. 30¢   18¢   87¢

135¢ or $1.35

How much would four trains cost? 87 x 4 = 80 x 4 + 7 x 4 = 320 + 28 = 348 = **$3.48**

D. Let's say you had five quarters and wanted to buy the train. How much do you
have left after you buy the train? You can remember that one dollar is just one
hundred cents. Three dollars and fifteen cents is 315 cents. You can add, subtract,
multiply, and divide money as just cents. Then change your answer back into
dollars. Your answer should match the problem. If the problem is in dollars, then
your answer should be in dollars and cents. Money always has two decimal places.

    $1.25   **$0.38**
  - $0.87
    125
    - 87
    100
    - 60
     - 2
     38

Now try it with these numbers. Buy the rubrics cube with $2.75. Buy the robot with $4.12. Buy sixteen boomerangs with $5.80.

$2.75 - $0.91 = 275 – 91 = 200 – 20 + 4 = 184 = **$1.84**

$4.12 - $0.59 = 412 – 59 = 400 – 40 – 7 = 353 = **$3.53**

First multiply $0.18 x 16 = 18 x 16 = 100 + 80 + 60 + 48 = 288 = $2.88
$5.80 - $2.88 = **$2.92**

Day 57
Make 100   (B: Intro to "borrowing")

The seed produced a hundredfold. (Matthew 13:18-23)

A.   We are going to make one hundred today, but we're going to start with making ten. If you had three of something, how many would you need to make ten?

7

How would you make ten if you had two, four, nine?

8, 6, 1

Now let's make 100. If you had 9, you need 1 to make ten. If you had 90, how many more do you need to get 100?

10

Make 100 with 30, 80, 20, 50, 40.

70, 20, 80, 50, 60

B.   To get from 4 to 10 you could subtract 10 – 4 to get 6. To get to 100 from 60 you can subtract 100 – 60 to get 40.

We're going to subtract in a new way today. What if I asked you to subtract 6 from 5? What would you do? Start at 5 on the number line and count down 6. What number do you end on?

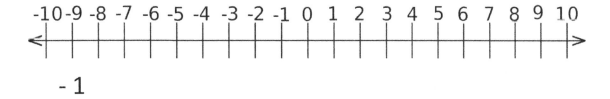

- 1

We call that negative one. It looks like minus one. That's just how we're going to use it, as minus one.

Let's say we're trying to get to 50. We have 31. Subtract 31 from 50 to see how much more we need.

     50
   - 31

We can subtract 50 minus 30 and get 20. What's the problem with taking 1 away from 0?

Start at 0 on the number line and take away one, go back one. What number do you end up on?

-1

So, when we subtract 50 minus 31, we get 20 and minus 1. What's 20 – 1? **19**

Try it with these numbers: 50 – 12, 50 – 24, 55 - 18

38, 26, 37
50 – 12 = 50 – 10 and 0 – 2 = 40 – 2 = 38 (2 and 8 make 10)
50 – 24 = 50 – 20 and 0 – 4 = 30 – 4 = 26 (4 and 6 make 10)
55 – 18 = 50 – 10 and 5 – 8 = 40 – 3 = 37 (3 and 7 make 10)
It doesn't matter what the ones digit is. You find the difference. If the number being subtracted is greater, the the answer is negative.

C.   Let's make 100. Let's subtract 100 – 41 together.

     100
   - 41
     100
   - 40
      60
   -   1
      59

You are basically subtracting 100 – 40 – 1. You can break up subtraction just like you can break up addition. If you subtract 40 and subtract 1 more, you are subtracting off 41. What's one hundred minus forty?

100 – 40 = 60 Just think about making ten. 10 – 4 = 6

60 – 1 = 59 Again, think about making ten. 10 – 1 = 9
(But in this case you are making 60, so it's not just 9, but 59.)

Make 100 out of these numbers: 59, 23, 74.

100 − 59 = 100 − 50 − 9 = 50 − 9 = **41** (1 and 9 make 10)
100 − 23 = 100 − 20 − 3 = 80 − 3 = **77** (7 and 3 make 10)
100 − 74 = 100 − 70 − 4 = 30 − 4 = **26** (6 and 4 make 10)

Now subtract from $1.00. It's the same thing. Can you see the 100 in there? Just drop the decimal straight down into the answer. A money answer will always have two decimal places, two digits after the decimal point. Think of these as 100.

$1.00
- $0.41
$0.59

Make $1.00 when you have 35 cents, sixty-eight cents, and 87 cents.

$0.65, $0.32, $0.13

NOTE: If you want to teach this the traditional way with borrowing, draw a box around the 1 and 0 to make a ten. Then cross it off and write nine above it. Add a one to the zero on the right to change that into ten ones. You can have them try these problems both ways to see what they prefer. When you are dealing with numbers like 100 and 1000, think of borrowing one from 10 and 100 (making them 9 and 99). It's easier than borrowing from each zero.

D.   Make 1000 when you have 20, 160, 390.

1000 − 20 = 1000 − 20 = 980 (2 and 8 make 10)
1000 − 160 = 1000 − 100 − 60 = 900 − 60 = 840 (1 and 9 make 10, 6 and 4 make 10)
1000 − 390 = 1000 − 300 − 90 = 700 − 90 = 610 (3 and 7 make 10, 1 & 9 make 10)

Make $10.00 when you have $1.30, $0.60, $7.05.

1000 − 130 = 1000 − 100 − 30 = 900 − 30 = 870 **$8.70**
1000 − 60 = 940 **$9.40**
1000 − 705 = 1000 − 700 − 5 = 300 − 5 = 295 **$2.95**

If you want to teach this the traditional way with borrowing, draw a box around the 1 and two 0s to make one hundred. Then cross it off and write ninety-nine above it. Add a one to the zero on the right to change that into ten ones. You can have them try these problems both ways.

Day 58
Geometry

The landowner planted seed in his field. (Matthew 13:24-30)

A.   We're going to draw the landowner's fields. He had a square field and a rectangular field. What's a square and what's a rectangle?

A square is a shape with four sides where each side is the same length. It has four equal sides and the four equally shaped corner angles. A rectangle is the same except that two of the sides are longer than the others.

Draw a square and a rectangle on the coordinate plane, the box below. Draw on the lines already there.

What's the perimeter and area of your square and rectangle? Remember that the perimeter is the measure around a shape and the area is the measure inside the shape. Count the boxes to find each.

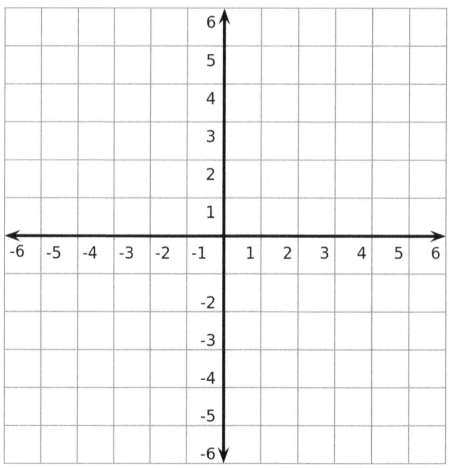

By H Padleckas via Wikimedia Commons

B. Find these points on the coordinate plane. The first number tells you the number going right and left and the second number tells you how many blocks up and down. (1,1) (-2,-2) (3, -5) (-4, 3)

The first one is over to the right one and up one. The second one is over to the left two blocks and then down two blocks.

Now write down the locations of the four corners of both your square and your rectangle. Write how many blocks over and how many blocks up or down. Remember, it's important to write the minus sign if it's going left or down.

answers will vary

If you did it correctly, there should be two coordinates the same for each of the first and second coordinates. How did I know that?

Squares and rectangles have parallel lines. They run straight across or straight up and down in the same way, not crooked compared to each other. Since they go straight, I knew they would stay on the same numbered line.

C. Use the coordinates to draw a trapezoid. Plot the points and then connect the dots. Then draw a congruent trapezoid and write its coordinates. A trapezoid is a shape with four sides. Two sides are of equal length. The other two sides are of different lengths and are parallel to each other. Congruent means the same size and shape. (0,0) (2,2) (3,2) (5,0)

answers will vary

D. Use the coordinates to draw a rhombus or a parallelogram. Then draw a congruent one and write its coordinates. A rhombus is like a square except that all four angles aren't equal. A parallelogram is a rectangle but all four angles aren't equal. The side lengths stay the same. The parallelogram has two sets of equal length sides and the rhombus has four equal sides. They are just kind of slanted, like the corners were on hinges and you pushed on one corner. Try drawing them in a blank spot before you draw them on the coordinate plane. You might want to use a ruler to make sure your sides stay equal length (as best you can).

Parallelogram: (0,0) (1,1) (4,1) (3,0)   Rhombus: (0,0) (2,0) (4,2) (2,0)

answers will vary

Day 59
Comparing Fractions, Fractions Arithmetic

The mustard seed grew until it was bigger than all the other plants. (Matthew 13:31-35)

A.   Let's figure out how much smaller the other plants were. The first rectangle is the mustard plant. Just pretend. That represents how big it is. Divide the next rectangle in half. Color in one half of it. Divide the next rectangle by four. (Draw two lines dividing it in half both ways.) Color in one quarter. Divide the last rectangle by three. Draw two lines to make three parts. Color in one third.

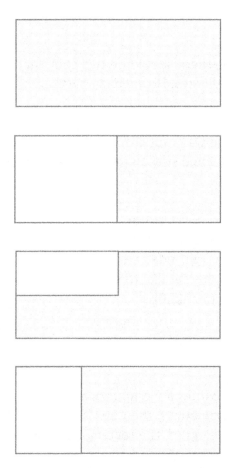

Use the greater than/less than symbol to show which is biggest in each pair.

1 > ¹/₃   ¹/₄ < ¹/₂

B.   How many halves would we need to make a whole?

2

Two plants, half the size, together would be the size of one mustard plant.

If you had 2 of the 2 halves, you would have the whole thing. If you want to see that, cut a piece of paper in half. You have one half and one half. If you put them together, you have two halves and one whole paper.

We write one half like this. $1/2$ The number on the bottom is how many parts there are all together. The top number tells us how many of the parts we're talking about.

We write two halves like this. $2/2$ That means we're talking about two of the two parts. If the top number matches the bottom number, what does that mean?

We have all the parts. We have the whole thing, 1 whole.

$2/2 = 1$ $100/100 = 1$ No matter what the numbers are, if the top number is the same as the bottom number, then there are all of the parts, one whole.

How many quarters do you need to make a half?

2

How do you write 2 out of 4 parts as a fraction?

$2/4$

How many quarters do you need to make a whole?

4

How do you write 4 out of 4 parts as a fraction?

$4/4$

What whole number (not a fraction) does $^4/_4$ equal?

1

What's bigger three fourths or one? Write your answer using < or >.

Three parts is less than four parts so $^3/_4$ < $^4/_4$ **meaning** $^3/_4$ < **1**

C.   Write an addition and a subtraction equation that give the answer $^3/_4$. Remember that three fourths just means three out of four parts. One part plus two parts equals three parts. The total number of parts never changes, the bottom number of the fraction. Just how many of the parts you have changes. You started with one part, added on two more parts, then you have three parts.

Answers can vary: $^1/_4$ + $^2/_4$ = $^3/_4$ **1 -** $^1/_4$ = $^3/_4$

Now write an addition equation and a subtraction equation with the answer $^3/_8$.

Answers can vary: $^1/_8$ + $^2/_8$ = $^3/_8$ **1 -** $^5/_8$ = $^3/_8$

How do you figure out one half of ten?

You would write that as an equation as one half times ten.

½ x 10   or   ½ (10)   or   ½ * 10   are all ways you can write it.

Look at the numbers: 1, 2, 10. How are those numbers being used to get 5 as the answer?

You are actually multiplying ten by one and dividing ten by two. When you divide ten things into two groups. You get five in each group. You have ten fingers but when you divide them into two hands, you end up with five fingers on each hand.

The equations I wrote gave the answer to a half of ten. Write an equation that would give you a quarter of sixteen.

$^1/_4$ (16)

D.   To solve $^1/_4$ (16) you would multiply sixteen times one and then divide by four. Or, you could divide sixteen by four and then multiply by one. It doesn't matter which order you do it in. What's the answer?

4

How would you solve $^3/_4$ (16)? What's the answer?

Sixteen divided by four is four. Four times three is twelve.

What's $^2/_5$ (35)?

14 $35 \div 5 = 7$ $7 \times 2 = 14$

Add one quarter and one half. Write the equation and answer.

$^1/_4 + ^2/_4 = ^3/_4$

Subtract one third from one. Write the equation and answer.

$1 - ^1/_3 = ^2/_3$ **same as** $^3/_3 - ^1/_3 = ^2/_3$

Day 60
Review

A.   How much are these coins worth? Match the coins to their values.

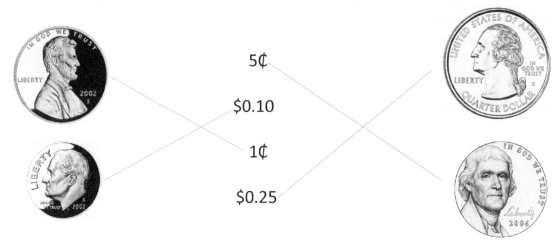

5¢

$0.10

1¢

$0.25

Pay for these items. (Use coins or paper coins.)

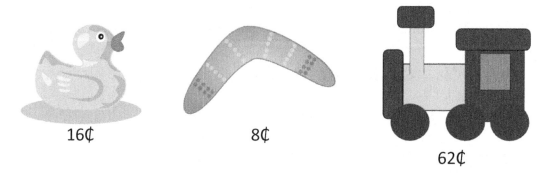

16¢   8¢

62¢

If one hundred cents equals one dollar, how many pennies do you need to make a dollar if you had forty already?

60 cents

Draw a square and a rectangle on the coordinate plane. Use the lines that are there and draw along those. What's the perimeter and area of your square and rectangle? Remember that the perimeter is the measure around a shape and the area is the measure inside the shape. Count the boxes to find each.

Use the greater than/less than symbol to show which is biggest in each pair.

1   >   1/2   1/4   <   1/3

B.   Use your coins to buy the items. How many ways can you pay for each item?

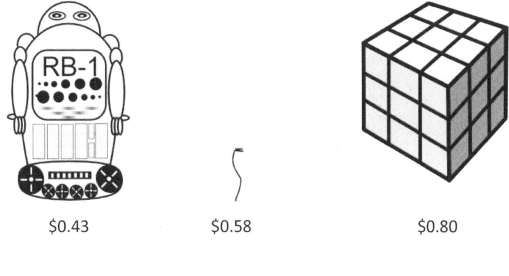

$0.43 $0.58 $0.80

```
   40          53          71
 - 12        - 26        - 52
 ─────       ─────       ─────
   30          30          20
  - 2         - 3         - 1
 ─────       ─────       ─────
   28          27          19
```

Draw a square and a rectangle on the coordinate plane and write down the coordinates of their corners.

Answers will vary.

What's bigger two thirds or one? Write your answer using < or >.

2/3 < 1   (One equals three thirds and two is less than three.)

C.   How much would four trains cost if one train was 75 cents?

75 x 4 = 70 x 4 and 5 x 4 = 280 + 20 = 300 = **$3.00**

Subtract.

$$\begin{array}{r} \$1.00 \\ - \$0.63 \\ \hline \mathbf{\$0.37} \end{array}$$
$$\begin{array}{r} \$1.00 \\ - \$0.38 \\ \hline \mathbf{\$0.62} \end{array}$$
$$\begin{array}{r} 100 \\ - 29 \\ \hline \mathbf{71} \end{array}$$

Draw a trapezoid and write its coordinates. Then draw a congruent one.

answers will vary

Write an addition equation and a subtraction equation that give the answer $5/7$.

Answers can vary: $2/7 + 3/7 = 5/7$ $1 - 2/7 = 5/7$

D.	Let's say you had five dimes, two quarters, and three nickels and wanted to buy the train toy for ninety-one cents. How much do you have left after you buy the train?

$1.15   **$0.24**
- $0.91
  115
  - 91
  100
  - 80
  + 4
   24

Make $10.00 when you have $6.28.

$3.72

Draw a parallelogram and write its coordinates. Then draw a congruent one.

answers will vary

What's $\frac{4}{7}$ (35)?

20   35 ÷ 7 = 5   5 x 4 = 20

Subtract one quarter from one. Write the equation and answer.

1 - $\frac{1}{4}$ = $\frac{3}{4}$

Days 61 - 70
Each workbook level has its own problems.

A.

Day 61
Addition: 18, 10, 13, 15, 9, 10
Addition: 39, 99, 50
Perimeter: 37
Calendar: 12 months

Day 62
Addition: 12, 9, 12, 17, 13, 12
Addition: 89, 75, 75
Perimeter: 15 blocks
Calendar: 7 days

Day 63
Subtraction: 8, 6, 7, 9, 5, 2
Subtraction: 17, 13, 0
Word problem: 7 workers
Word problem: 62 workers
Money: $1

Day 64
Subtraction: 6, 7, 5, 3, 7, 8
Subtraction: 43, 12, 100
Word problem: 1/2
Word problem: 140 steps

Day 65
Play store

A.

Day 66
Addition: 9, 11, 15, 11, 13, 12
Addition: 99, 88, 100
Rounding: 30, 70, 80, 30
Word problem: 70 miles
Greater than/Less than: >, >

Day 67
Addition: 12, 10, 13, 12, 16, 12
Addition: 37, 57, 490
Word problem: 110 miracles
Greater than/Less than: <, >

Day 68
Subtraction: 9, 5, 6, 9, 9, 8
Subtraction: 15, 51, 50
Word problem: 5 hours
Negative numbers: 2

Day 69
Subtraction: 7, 5, 5, 8, 9, 9
Subtraction: 30, 21, 50
Double: 6, 60, 600
Blanks: 7, 8, 40, 8
Money: 30 cents

Day 70
Play store

B.

Day 61
Addition: 80, 80, 60, 78, 90, 62
Perimeter: 52 miles
Area: 50 blocks
Angles: All the way around, halfway around, a quarter of the way around

Day 62
Addition: 218, 419, 573, 228
Calendar: 52 weeks
Calendar: 122 days

Day 63
Subtraction: 39, 47, 19, 38
Word problem: 83 workers
Word problem: 90 workers

Day 64
Subtraction: 17, 79, 25, 46
Money: 18 cents
Fractions: ¼
Fractions: ¾

Day 65
Subtraction: 19, 25, 18, 12

B.

Day 66
Addition: 589, 895, 309, 257
Word problem: 75 flights
Rounding: 20, 40, 50, 30
Estimation: 140 km
Greater than/Less than: 2/3 < 1

Day 67
Addition: 138, 103, 120, 125, 103, 92
Estimation: 70 miracles
Greater than/Less than: <, 130 < 132

Day 68
Subtraction: 18, 48, 21, 9
Word problem: 2:30
Negative numbers: 31

Day 69
Subtraction: 28, 7, 32, 39
Word problems: 80 pieces
Subtraction: 800
Blanks: 34, 36

Day 70
Play store

C.

Day 61
Perimeter: 1585 cm.
Area: 2660 in²
Protractor: three lines

Day 62
Arithmetic: 483, 60, 853, 63
Multiply: 2340 minutes
Word problem: 102 workers

Day 63
Arithmetic: 1243, 700, 1205, 42
Money: $4.07
Fractions: 6/11 >5/11

Day 64
Arithmetic: 838, 96, 405, 38
Word problem: 6552 steps
Rounding: 100, 700, 200, 500
Fractions: Answers will vary. Examples: 9/11 − 1/11 = 8/11, 3/11 + 5/11 = 8/11

Day 65
Line one: 1557, 420, 1144, 471
Line two: 1243, 700, 846, 42
Line three: 1585, 870, 1156

C.

Day 66
Arithmetic: 661, $0.70, 563, $0.52
Estimation: 120 − 50 = 70 miles
Estimation: 200 x 6 = 1200, 240 x 6 = 1440, 238 x 6 = 1428 miracles

Day 67
Arithmetic: 673, $0.20, 1051, $0.64
Greater than/Less than: > 2776 >2490
Time 6 hours and 18 minutes

Day 68
Arithmetic: 1000, $7.00, 966, $0.29
Negative numbers: 206
Word problem: 42,000 pieces of fruit
Blanks: 213 (154 + 59), 456 (620 − 164)

Day 69
Word problem: $3.72
Arithmetic: 1075, $0.40, 282, $0.62
Geometry: answers will vary

Day 70
Line one: 788, 700, 1026, $0.71
Line two: 375, 900, 1084, $0.83
Line three: 2140, 1536, 1520

D.

Day 61
Graph: Answers will vary. The area is the number of blocks inside of the trapezoid. You should count up half blocks along with whole blocks. The coordinates are written (x,y). The first number is the number right or left. The second number shows where it is vertically. Left and down are shown by negative numbers.
Perimeter: 1435 units

Day 62
Arithmetic: 2371, $4.60, 8263, $5.13
Word problem: 210 – 91 = $1.19
Multiplying by fractions: 27
Fractions: 3/3 – 1/3 = 2/3

Day 63
Arithmetic: 1324, $610, 10,233 ; $8.64
Multiplying fractions: 60
Multiply: 14,945 ; 25,241

Day 64
Arithmetic: 3107, $7.30 ; 10,273 ; $6.84
Word problem: 288 – 75 = 213 difference with 671 = 458 workers
Blanks: 23, 1100

Day 65
Arithmetic: 8065, $6.40 ; 30,810 ; $5.28
Multiplying by fractions: 108
Divide: 85

D.

Day 66
Word problem: 37 x 24 = 888 stairs
Rounding: 400, 100, 900, 1000
Multiplying by fractions: 325
Divide: 35

Day 67
Multiply: 6,000,000 (6 million)
Divide: 600,000
Estimation: 200 + 400 + 300 = 900 minutes = 15 hours, 200 + 360 + 280 = 840 minutes = 14 hours, 200 + 364 + 276 = 840 minutes = 14 hours
Multiplying by fractions: 234
Divide: 48

Day 68
Negative numbers: 246
Estimation: 200 ÷ 4 = 50 miracles, 160 ÷ 4 = 40 miracles, 164 ÷ 4 = 41 miracles
Multiplying by fractions: 325
Divide: 35

Day 69
Greater than/Less than: 2028 (wheat) < 2596 (barley)
Time: 9 hours and 27 minutes

Day 70
Arithmetic: 4040, $5.84; 14,868 ; $4.28
Multiplying fractions: 324
Divide: 46

Day 71
Roman Numerals

Jesus was transfigured. (Matthew 17:1-8)

A.   We're going to transfigure numbers today and change them into Roman numerals.

      The capital letter I represents the number 1. What number do you think is III?

      3

      The capital letter V represents the number 5. What number do you think is VI?

      6

      The capital letter X represents the number 10. What number do you think is XV?

      15

      Figure out what these numbers are:

      VII = **7**   XVI = **16**   II = **2**   XIII = **13**

B.   If VI is 6, what do you think is IV?

      4

      To keep numbers from getting really long, sometimes you subtract instead of add. If the lesser number comes before the greater number, you subtract it. Otherwise, the bigger number always comes first.

      XVI is ten, five, one or sixteen. What's XIV?

      14

      Figure out these numbers:

      XX = **20**   IX = **9**   XIX = **19**   XIV = **14**

C. Let's learn more letters. L = 50 and C = 100 What would be XL?

40 It's 50 – 10.

For thirty you would write XXX. You only write three in a row of something. Once you need to make 4 or 40, 9 or 90, then you subtract and put the smaller number first.

How would you write 300?

CCC

How would you write 150, 190, 340, and 280?

CL, CXC, CCLIII

D. Learn two more letters. D = 500 and M = 1000 What would be 1984 in Roman numerals?

MCMLXXXIV

How would you write these numbers?

2017, 570, 499, 1238

MMXVII, DLXX, CDXCIX, MCCXXXVIII
You can't write ID for 499. You have to write out each number: 400, 90, 9.

Day 72 (ruler)
Measuring

Jesus and his disciples were coming down the mountain. (Matthew 17:9-18)

A.   Jesus and his disciples were coming down the mountain. Can you draw a mountain on your page that's an inch high? How about three centimeters? Which is higher? (Note: Show your child how to start at the zero and to measure to the line by the number.)

3 centimeters

B.   Draw a mountain or a line that's three and a half inches long. Then draw one that is six and a half centimeters long. Which is longer? (Note: Show your child the longer halfway mark on the ruler between the numbered measurements.)

3.5 inches

C.   Measure five things in your house and write down their measurement in centimeters. There are ten lines for each centimeter. We can write tenths like this.

0.1 one tenth, 0.2 two tenths, 0.3 three tenths, etc. Each line is one tenth. Just count them up. If it measured seven centimeters and then eight more little lines, the answer would be 7.8.

D.   Measure five things in your house and write down their measurement in inches. You'll use fractions this time. There are sixteen lines for each inch.

8 lines would be $8/16$ or ½

4 lines would be $4/16$ or ¼

2 lines would be $2/16$ or $1/8$

3 lines would be $3/16$

If it measured 5 inches and 5 little lines, the answer would be 5 $5/16$. That's called a mixed number when the number is part whole number and part fraction.

Day 73
Decimals

The disciples' faith is little. (Matthew 17:19-27)

A.   The disciples' faith is little. Oh no! What if we could measure it? How big do you think it was? Today we're going to look at small numbers.

Draw ten circles. Color in one.

We write 0.1 when we write that as a decimal. The little dot we call a decimal point. We read it one tenth. That means one of the ten.

Color in one more circle. How do you think you would write two tenths as a decimal?

0.2

Color in four more circles. Write as a decimal sixth tenths.

0.6

B.   Fractions and decimals are different ways to write the same number.

To write one tenth, 0.1, as a fraction you write one over ten.

Write three tenths as a fraction and decimal.

³/₁₀   0.3

Write seven tenths and nine tenths as fractions and decimals.

⁷/₁₀   0.7   ⁹/₁₀   0.9

C.   How do you say this number: 0.1?

one tenth

How do you think you write the number one and one tenth as a decimal?

1.1

How do you think you write that as a fraction?

1 $1/10$

Write three and seven tenths and eight and three tenths as decimals and fractions.

3.7   3 $7/10$ 8.3   8 $3/10$

D.   What fraction is this $1/100$? That's the value of one penny. It's one out of one hundred cents.

one hundredth

It is one hundredth or one one hundredth. What does it mean?

It means one part out of one hundred.

What is one hundredth of a dollar? (Hint: A dollar is how many cents?)

a penny

What is the value of a nickel as a fraction of one hundred? A dime?

$5/100$ $10/100$

We've learned place value such as hundreds, tens, and ones. After the decimal point comes tenths. A one in that spot means one tenth. Next comes the hundredths. A one in that place means one hundredth.

hundreds tens ones . tenths hundredths

Write the value of a penny, a nickel, a dime, and a quarter as decimals. As examples: 0.02 is two out of one hundred or two cents and 0.7 is 7 tens out of one hundred. Seven tens is 70 out of 100, which is 70 cents.

0.01, 0.05, 0.10, 0.25

Day 74
Fractions/Decimals

Jesus tells the disciples to be converted. (Matthew 18:1-6)

A.   We're going to convert fractions into decimals. Follow the pattern to convert the fractions into decimals.

$\frac{1}{10}$ $\frac{2}{10}$ $\frac{3}{10}$ $\frac{4}{10}$ $\frac{5}{10}$ $\frac{6}{10}$ $\frac{7}{10}$ $\frac{8}{10}$ $\frac{9}{10}$

0.1   0.2   0.3   0.4   **0.5**   **0.6**   **0.7**   **0.8**   **0.9**

B.   Do the opposite. Convert the decimals into fractions.

0.1   0.2   0.3   0.4   0.5   0.6   0.7   0.8   0.9

$\frac{1}{10}$ $\frac{2}{10}$ $\frac{3}{10}$ $\frac{4}{10}$ $\frac{5}{10}$ $\frac{6}{10}$ $\frac{7}{10}$ $\frac{8}{10}$ $\frac{9}{10}$

C.   Write these numbers as decimals and then convert them to mixed numbers (where there is a whole number and a fraction together): seven and one tenth, eight and seven tenths, twelve and nine tenths, five and five tenths.

7.1 $7\frac{1}{10}$ 8.7 $8\frac{7}{10}$ 12.9 $12\frac{9}{10}$ 5.5 $5\frac{5}{10}$

Compare the first two and the last two numbers (that you just wrote). Draw a greater than and less than symbol between them.

7.1 < 8.7   12.9 > 5.5

What else does five out of ten equal? How else could you write five tenths and have it mean the same amount?

Five is half of ten, so five tenths equals one half. You can write one half.

D.   Write as decimals 57 hundredths, 4 and 17 hundredths, 28 and 3 hundredths, 189 and 9 tenths. Compare the first two numbers and the last two numbers.

0.57   <   4.17   28.03   <   189.9

Now convert them to fractions or mixed numbers.

$\frac{57}{100}$ $4\frac{17}{100}$ $28\frac{3}{100}$ $189\frac{9}{10}$

Day 75
Review

The apostles were sent out as sheep among wolves. (Matthew 10:16-25)

A.   What are these numbers?

VI = **6**   XV = **15**   III = **3**   XI = **11**

Draw a line that is six centimeters long.

Draw ten lines. Circle three of them. Write that as a decimal, 3 of 10 or three tenths.

0.3

Follow the pattern to convert the fractions into a decimals.

$^1/_{10}$ $^2/_{10}$ $^3/_{10}$ $^4/_{10}$ $^5/_{10}$ $^6/_{10}$ $^7/_{10}$ $^8/_{10}$ $^9/_{10}$
0.1   **0.2**   0.3   **0.4**   0.5   **0.6**   0.7   **0.8**   0.9

B.   What numbers are these?

IX = **9**   IV = **4**   XXIX = **29**   XV = **15**

Draw a line that's four and a half inches long. Then draw one that is eight and a half centimeters long. Which is longer? (Note: Show your child the longer halfway mark on the ruler between the numbered measurements.)

4.5 inches

Write three tenths and one tenth as fractions and decimals.

$3/10$ 0.3   **$1/10$ 0.1**

Convert the decimals into fractions or the fractions into decimals.

0.1   0.2   0.3   0.4   0.5   **0.6**   **0.7**   **0.8**   **0.9**
$1/10$ **$2/10$** **$3/10$** **$4/10$** **$5/10$** $6/10$ $7/10$ $8/10$ $9/10$

C.   How would you write 140, 250, and 139?

CXL, CCL, CXXXIX

Measure five things in your house and write down their measurement in centimeters. Use a decimal.

.

Write four and three tenths and five and seven tenths as decimals and fractions.

4.3 4 3/10   5.7 5 7/10

Write these numbers as decimals and then convert them to fractions: six and one tenth, two and seven tenths, twenty and nine tenths.

6.1 6 1/10   2.7 2 7/10   20.9 20 9/10

Compare these numbers and draw a greater than and less than symbol between the sets of numbers.

7.9 < 8.1   12 > 10.8

D.   How would you write these numbers?

1999, 870, 400, 1478

MCMXCIX, DCCCLXX, CD, MCDLXXVIII

Measure five things in your house and write down their measurement in inches. You'll use fractions this time. There are sixteen lines for each inch. Write mixed numbers if the measurement is over one, and write the fractions in the lowest terms, such as eight sixteenths equals one half. You can use your page on Day 71 to help you.

Write the value of a penny, a nickel, a dime, and a quarter as decimals.

0.01, 0.05, 0.10, 0.25

Write as decimals 67 hundredths, 1 and 1 hundredth, 280 and 9 hundredths, 289 and 3 tenths. Compare the first two numbers and the last two numbers.

0.67   <   1.01   280.09   <   289.3

Now convert them to fractions.

$^{67}/_{100}$ $1\,^{1}/_{100}$ $280\,^{9}/_{100}$ $289\,^{3}/_{10}$

Day 76
Numbers – Place Value

Two or three witnesses are needed and Jesus is in the midst of where two or three are gathered. (Matthew 18:15-20)

A. We're going to read and write numbers today. Write these numbers and then read them out loud.

hundreds | tens | ones

six hundred seventy-four **674**
eight hundred five **805**
three hundred twenty-nine **329**
one hundred fifty **150**

B. Write these numbers and then read them out loud.

thousand , hundreds | tens | ones

one thousand three hundred **1,300**
four thousand two hundred ninety-two **4,292**
eight thousand five hundred one **8,501**
nine thousand fifty **9,050**

C. Write these numbers and then read them out loud. Whether you are talking about trillions or thousands, place value for each always goes hundreds, tens, then ones. Between each set of hundreds/tens/ones, we place a comma.

hundred thousand | ten thousand | one thousand , hundreds | tens | ones

twenty-five thousand, six hundred seventy **25,670**
fifty-one thousand, twenty-four **51,024**
one hundred thousand one **100,001**
four hundred sixty-one thousand, three hundred eighty-seven **461,387**

D. Write these numbers and then read them out loud.

millions , hundred thousand | ten thousand | thousand , hundreds | tens | ones

six hundred seventeen thousand four **617,004**
eight hundred thousand four hundred twelve **800,412**
one million forty-two thousand six hundred fifteen **1,042,615**
eleven million five hundred thousand three hundred nine **11,500,309**

Day 77
Multiplication

We should forgive seventy times seven. (Matthew 18:21-27)

A.   We're going to multiply today. Let's try ten times seven. Go to the table on Day 7 and put your finger on ten. Count by ten seven times. What's seven times ten?

70

Count by tens and find 3 times 10, 4 times 10, 8 times 10, 10 times 10.

30, 40, 80, 100

B.   Multiply.

20 x 5 = **100**   3 x 20 = **60**

15 x 10 = **150**   25 x 8 = **200**
                                    Think quarters. How much is 25 cents four times?

C.   Multiply.

14 x 35 = 14 x 30 and 14 x 5 = 300 + 120 and 50 + 20 = 420 + 70 = **490**

46 x 29 = 40 x 29 and 6 x 29 = 800 + 360 and 120 + 54 = 1160 and 174 = **1334**

28 x 71 = 20 x 71 and 8 x 71 = 1400 + 20 and 560 + 8 = 1420 + 568 = **1988**

39 x 67 = 30 x 67 and 9 x 67 = 1800 + 210 and 540 + 63 = 2010 + 603 = **2613**

D.   Multiply.

123 x 45 = 100 x 45 and 20 x 45 and 3 x 45 = 4500 and 800 + 100 and 120 + 15 = 4500 + 900 + 135 = **5535**

241 x 68 = **16388**

315 x 74 = **23310**

239 x 45 = **10755**

Day 78
Subtraction, Negative Numbers

The men are in debt. (Matthew 18:28-35)

A.   Let's say you just got ten dollars as a present from your aunt. However, you owe
      your parents five dollars that you borrowed to buy a present. After you pay them
      back, how much money will you have? How would you figure that out?

      10 – 5 = 5 dollars

      Now let's look at it a different way. You started with a debt of five dollars. Where
      would that be on the number line?

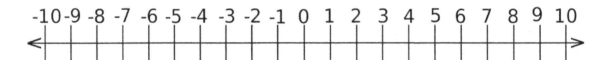

      It would have to be the negative five because it doesn't make sense if it were the
      five. That would mean you had five dollars. But you have the opposite of that. You
      owe five dollars.

      Put your finger on the negative five. We write it – 5, like minus 5. Now add on the
      ten dollar gift. Count up ten.

      What's the answer?

      5

B.   You just solved -5 + 10 = 5. Do you see how that's related to 10 – 5 = 5?

      They are the same thing, just reversed, and we didn't write the plus sign next to
      the ten in the second equation. Every number is either positive or negative, except
      for zero. We just don't write a plus + sign next to the positive ones. We like to keep
      things simple, and it's easiest to just assume numbers are positive unless we write
      the negative.

      When we subtract, we're just adding a negative number. Cool, right?

Add. (Remember that adding a negative number is just subtracting it. You can reverse the problems and rewrite them if you need to.)

$-6 + 12 = \mathbf{6}$ $-7 + 16 = \mathbf{9}$
$-4 + 11 = \mathbf{7}$ $-8 + 14 = \mathbf{6}$

You have twenty five dollars of debt and just got one hundred thirty-two dollars from a job you completed. How much money do you have after you paid off your debt?

$-25 + 132 = 132 - 25 = 100 + 10 - 3 = \mathbf{107\ dollars}$

What if you had 52 dollars of debt and got in 271 dollars?

$-52 + 271 = 271 - 52 = 200 + 20 - 1 = 220 - 1 = \mathbf{219\ dollars}$

C.   Add and subtract.

Let's say you had fifty-two dollars of debt and got two hundred thirty-seven dollars. How much money would you have after you paid your debt? (Note: You could walk through the first one together, subtracting the hundreds, then the tens, then the ones.)

$-52 + 237 = 237 - 52 = 200 - 20 + 5 = 180 + 5 = \mathbf{185\ dollars}$
Take it step by step. If you combined 20 and 5 first, then you would end up subtracting 25 instead of 20. You need to make sure you are subtracting 20 and adding five to the total.

```
237     You can also subtract like this. Subtract everything you can without
- 52    "borrowing" and then subtract off the negative.
205
- 20
```

What if you had forty-two dollars of debt and got eight hundred three dollars? How much money would you have after you paid your debt?

$-42 + 803 = 803 - 42 = 800 - 40 + 1 = \mathbf{761\ dollars}$

Try it with these numbers: $150 of debt and receiving $429 dollars, $480 dollars of debt and receiving $800.

```
429                429
- 150              - 150
 300               309    with doing all the "positives" first
- 30              - 30
+ 9    You don't have to write the plus, but it's a good habit until it comes
 279   naturally.
$279
```

```
 800
- 480
 400
- 80
+ 0    There's no reason to write out the plus zero. I'm just showing the steps
 320   because if there had been something there, you would be adding or
$320   subtracting it on.
```

D.   Let's say you had five hundred thirty-two dollars of debt and got two thousand dollars. How much money would you have after you paid your debt? (Note: You could walk through the first one together, subtracting the thousands, then the hundreds, then the tens, then the ones.)

$$-532 + 2000 = 2000 - 532 = 2000 - 500 - 30 - 2 = 1500 - 30 - 2 = 1470 - 2 = \mathbf{1468}$$
Writing out the steps prevents mistakes.

How much money would have after you paid back a debt of $19.38 if you had $25.70? (Hint: Just ignore the decimal point to subtract, but make sure it stays in the same place in the answer. Drop it straight down into the answer. There should be two decimal places to the right of the decimal point.)

$$\$25.70 - \$19.38 = 2570 - 1938 = 1000 - 400 + 40 - 8 = 600 + 32 = 632 => \mathbf{\$6.32}$$

Try it with these numbers: $5023 and $1531, $62.01 and $17.58.

```
5023         5023                        $62.01        6201
- 1531       -1531                       - $17.58      -1758
4000         4002                         5000         5000
-500         3502  (-500)                - 500         4500
-10          3492  (-10)                 -50          4450
+2           There is more than one      - 7          4443
3500         way to find the answer     $44.43
- 10         This way keeps track of
+2           the totals after you subtract.
3492         You wouldn't write the (-500) part.
```

Day 79
Whole numbers, Fractions, B: Mixed Numbers, D: Improper fractions

What God has put together let no man separate. (Matthew 19:1-15)

A.   We are going to take apart numbers today. God doesn't mind that. When we talk about numbers, we're really referring to whole numbers. Numbers like 0, 1, 2, 3, 4, 5, 6, 7, 100, 3000, etc. Those are all whole numbers.

What's a whole number that's even, larger than twelve and less than fifteen?

14

What's a fraction?

It's part of a whole number.

Draw a picture of a circle and divide it in half. How much is each side of the circle?

½

Now put both sides together. How much are they together?

1, one whole circle, one whole number

A fraction is part of a whole number. How many fractions are there?

an infinite amount
You could keep cutting that circle into more and more pieces if you had a microscopic paper cutter. You could have one one millionth as a fraction. You could have one one trillionth as a fraction. That would mean one of out a trillion pieces.

What fraction is exactly in the middle of the whole numbers 0 and 1?

½

B.   Draw four circles. Draw a line to divide one of them in half.

Color in one half of the circle. How much is uncolored?

3 and ½

We write 3 ½ like this. It's called a mixed number. Why is that its name?

It's made up of a whole number and a fraction.

Write these as mixed numbers: four and one tenth, twelve and two thirds, one hundred and three quarters.
4 1/10, 12 2/3, 100 ¾

C.   Draw a line through the other three circles. Now write how many halves are uncolored.

$^{7}/_{2}$

Draw three boxes. Divide them into quarters. Color one quarter of one box. Write the amount uncolored two ways. (Hint: One should be a mixed number.)

2 ¾ , $^{11}/_{4}$

The mixed number isn't anything mysterious. It's just a whole number and then a part of another. It's 2 and ¾ , but we can combine them and write them as one number called an improper fraction. An improper fraction is when the numerator, the top number, is greater than the denominator, the bottom number.

Add together six and one third and twelve and one third. (Hint: You can break them apart to add.)

6 1/3 + 12 1/3 = 6 + 1/3 + 12 + 1/3 = 6 + 12 + 1/3 + 1/3 = 18 + 2/3 = **18 $^{2}/_{3}$**

Add together four and three fourths and two and one forth.

4 + ¾ + 2 + ¼ = 6 + 4/4 = 6 + 1 = **7**

D.   Draw a picture to show both two and a half and three and three quarters. Write each as a mixed number and an improper fraction (where the numerator, the top number is bigger than the denominator, the bottom number). Next, add the improper fractions. Stop! To do that you have to be adding things with the same number of pieces. How can you turn the half into four pieces so that the denominators will be the same? (You can use your pictures to help you.) Then get back to the original direction of adding together the improper fractions. Finally, write the answer as a mixed number. (You can use your pictures to help you.)

2 ½ and 3 ¾
$^{5}/_{2}$ and $^{15}/_{4}$
$^{10}/_{4}$ + $^{15}/_{4}$ = $^{25}/_{4}$ = 6 $^{1}/_{4}$

Day 80
Review

A.   Write these numbers and then read them out loud.

three hundred sixty-five
nine hundred and twelve

365, 912

Find 6 times 10, 5 times 10, and 11 times 10.

60, 50, 110

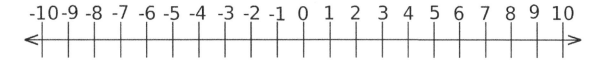

Start with a debt of four dollars. Get a gift of nine dollars. Count up the number line to see how much money you have left after you pay your debt.

5

Draw a rectangle. Draw two lines across it to divide it into three parts. Color in one of the parts. Which of these fractions describes the picture you drew?

$\frac{1}{2}$ $\boxed{\frac{1}{3}}$ $\frac{1}{4}$

B.   Write these numbers and then read them out loud.

five thousand three hundred ninety
eight thousand thirty-four

Multiply.

12 x 10 = **120**   25 x 6 = **150**

Add. (Remember that adding a negative number is just subtracting it. You can reverse the problems and rewrite them if you need to.)

$-7 + 13 = 6$ $-8 + 15 = 7$

You have twenty five dollars of debt and just got three hundred and eighty-three dollars from a job you completed. How much money do you have after you paid if your debt?

$-25 + 383 = 383 - 25 = 300 + 60 - 2 = 300 + 58 =$ **358 dollars**

Write these as mixed numbers: four and three tenths, twenty and two thirds, one hundred forty and one quarter.

$4\,^3/_{10}$, $20\,^2/_3$, $140\,¼$

C. Write these numbers and then read them out loud.

hundred thousand | ten thousand | one thousand , hundreds | tens | ones

twenty-three thousand, six hundred seven
one hundred fifty thousand, one hundred and fourteen

23,607
150,114

Multiply.

34 x 51 = 30 x 51 and 4 x 51 = 1500 + 30 and 200 + 4 = 1530 + 204 = **1734**

29 x 87 = 20 x 87 and 9 x 87 = 1600 + 140 and 720 + 63 = 1740 + 783 = **2523**

Let's say you had fifty-two dollars of debt and got in five hundred and twenty-six dollars. How much money would you have after you paid your debt?

− 52 + 526 = 526 − 52 = 500 − 30 + 4 =470 + 4 = **474 dollars**
You have to work left to right. If you combined 30 and 4 first, then you would end up subtracting 34 instead of 30.

$$\begin{array}{r} 700 \\ -\ 241 \\ \hline 500 \end{array}$$

$$\begin{array}{r} -\ 40 \quad 460 \\ -\ 1 \\ \hline \mathbf{459} \end{array}$$

Add together three and one third and fifteen and one third.

3 1/3 + 15 1/3 = 3 + 1/3 + 15 + 1/3 = 3 + 15 + 1/3 + 1/3 = 18 + 2/3 = **18 $^2/_3$**

D. Write these numbers and then read them out loud.

millions , hundred thousand | ten thousand | thousand , hundreds | tens | ones

nine hundred twenty thousand, four hundred and two
eleven million five hundred ninety-five thousand and eighteen

920,402
11,595,018

Multiply. (Reminder: 500 x 30 has three zeros in the answer.)

567 x 32 = 500 x 32 and 60 x 32 and 7 x 32 = 15000 + 1000 and 1800 + 120 and 210
+ 14 = 17,000 + 1100 + 40 + 4 = **18,144**

Let's say you had four hundred fifty-six dollars of debt and got two thousand
dollars. How much money would you have after you paid your debt?

$- 456 + 2000 = 2000 - 456 = 2000 - 400 - 50 - 6 = 1600 - 50 - 6 = 1550 - 6 = \textbf{1544}$

$$
\begin{array}{rl}
4083 & \\
- 1335 & \\
\hline
3000 & \\
-300 & \\
+ 50 & \\
- 2 & \\
\hline
2700 & \\
+ 48 & \\
\hline
\textbf{2748} &
\end{array}
$$

$$
\begin{array}{l}
\$31.48 \\
- \$17.50 \\
\hline
2000 \\
- 600 \\
-10 \\
+ 8 \\
\hline
1400 \rightarrow 1390 \rightarrow 1398 \rightarrow \$13.98
\end{array}
$$

Draw a picture to show both one and a third and three and one sixth. Write each
as a mixed number and an improper fraction. Next, add the improper fractions.
Stop! To do that you have to be adding things with the same number of pieces.
How can you turn the third into six pieces so that the denominators will be the
same? (You can use your pictures to help you.) Then get back to the original
direction of adding together the improper fractions. Finally, write the answer as a
mixed number. (You can use your pictures to help you.)

$1\,{}^1/_3$ and $3\,{}^1/_6$ ${}^4/_3$ and ${}^{19}/_6$ ${}^8/_6$ + ${}^{19}/_6$ = ${}^{27}/_6$ = $4\,{}^3/_6$ = $4\,{}^1/_2$

Day 81 (A: at least five pennies, two nickels, one dime, B and C: lots of coins)
Money

The workers were each paid a denarius. (Matthew 20:1-7)

A.   We're going to get a dime, ten cents. This is how you write ten cents.

10 ¢ or $0.10

This is how you write five cents and one cent.

5 ¢ or $0.05   and   1 ¢ or $0.01

Use the coins to make ten cents in three different ways. For instance. You can make five cents by adding $0.01 + $0.01 + $0.01 + $0.01 + $0.01.

Write down five cents plus five cents equals ten cents in a different way.

5 ¢ + 5 ¢ = 10 ¢ $0.05 + $0.05 = $0.10

B.   We're going to pay the workers a dollar. Use coins to come up with five different ways to add coins together to get one dollar.

Combine coins that equal a dollar into two piles. Write down at least two equations. Use a dollar sign. Example: $0.50 + $0.50 = $1.00

Then write two subtraction equations using what you just wrote.
Example: $1.00 - $0.50 = $0.50

C.   To subtract from one dollar, you need to be able to subtract from 100. Do you see the similarity? 100 and $1.00

When we add and subtract with money, we can just act like we are using normal numbers. We just need to be careful to make sure we write our answer as money.

$2.13   We add this like 213 and 149. 300 + 50 + 12 = 362

+ $1.49   So, what's the answer? Write it in your workbook.

$.   **$3.62**

Now let's talk about subtracting from 10. What's 10 – 4? **6** What's 20 – 4? **16** What's 30 – 4? **26** What's 70 – 4? **66** What's 100 – 4? **96**

It's like going up one row on the hundreds chart and then figuring out 10 – 4.

What's 100 – 40? Look at the example below. It's just like subtracting 10 – 4. Can you see it?

```
100        100
- 40       - 43
 60         60
            - 3
            57
```

What's $1.00 - $0.40? **$0.60**

What's $1.00 - $0.43? **$0.57**

Subtract. Then check to see if your answers make sense! Add the answer and what you subtracted together, even use coins to do it. Do they make a dollar?

$1.00	$1.00	$1.00	$1.00	$1.00
-$0.30	-$0.53	-$0.78	-$0.16	-$0.24
$0.70	**$0.47**	**$0.22**	**$0.84**	**$0.76**

D.   Add and subtract. Then check to see if your answers make sense.

$0.90	$5.00	$1.18	$10.00	$6.50
+$0.30	-$1.29	+$0.88	- $0.46	+$3.74
$1.20	**$3.71**	**$2.06**	**$9.54**	**$10.24**

Day 82
Working with Money

They were each paid a denarius. (Matthew 20:8-16)

A.   The workers are getting their pay. How much would they get paid if they got paid fifty cents? Write that two ways. (You can look back at Day 81 for help.)

50¢ $0.50

Write these amounts in dollars and cents: 25 cents, 72 cents, 10 cents plus 8 cents, 12 cents minus 9 cents. (Note: They are to write the answers, not the equations.)

25¢ $0.25   **72¢ $0.72**   **18¢ $0.18**   **3¢ $0.03**

B.   Write how much the workers were paid if they were paid three dollars and forty-five cents.

$3.45

Write these amounts in dollars and cents: five dollars plus five dollars, twelve dollars and ten cents plus twenty dollars and twenty-five cents, thirty-eight dollars and sixty-four cents minus five dollars and thirty cents. (Note: Encourage them to think 12 apples + 10 apples is 22 apples, so 12 dollars and 10 dollars is 22 dollars. The same goes for cents.)

$10.00 , $22.35 , $33.34

C.   Write in dollars what is fifty-six cents plus forty-eight cents.

$1.04
56 + 48 = 90 + 14 = 104

How much would five workers get paid all together if they got paid these different amounts?

Amounts: five dollars and fifty-five cents, thirteen dollars and forty cents, twenty-six dollars and seventy cents, forty-six dollars and fifteen cents, one hundred five dollars and six cents.

(Note: You can figure out the dollars and cents separately and then combine them. Every 100 cents = 1 dollar. You could also write them without the money symbols, such as $15.55 = 1555 cents.)

$196.86

D.   Of course, that's not what happened. They each got paid the same amount. Multiply each amount by five to find out how much the five workers got paid all together. Try it with these amounts:

$12.05, $5.78, $53.40, $1.96

$60.25, $28.90, $267.00, $9.80

Day 83
Multiplication

Jesus said he would be scourged. (Matthew 20:17-23)

A.   When Jesus was beaten, he wasn't just whipped. He was scourged. It was a special whip with multiple strands attached to it. When the guard whipped Him once, He might have actually been cut three times, five times, ten times. I don't really want to talk about Jesus getting beaten, so let's multiply without the word problem today.

Let's multiply by three and five today. What's three four times? Count by threes while counting with tally marks to four. Say the first three and make a tally mark, a little line on the page. Then count on three more and say six and make another tally mark. That is three two times so far. Keep going.

12

What's three times six?

18

Count by fives with tally marks to figure out five times five and five times seven.

25, 35

B.   Use tally marks to ten to figure out what is one half times ten.

½ , 1, 1 ½, 2, 2 ½, 3, 3 ½, 4, 4 ½, **5**

What's one half times eight? What's one half times twelve?

4, 6

What's the pattern?

They are just half the number.

Multiplying by ½ is the same as dividing by two or finding half the number. So, what's 20 times ½?

10

What's 10 x 1, 10 x 0, and 10 x 10?

10, 0, 100

Everything times one, everything one time is the same number. Anything times zero, anything zero times, is just zero. Anything times ten is that number with a zero added onto it.

C.   Multiply.

340 x 25 = 6000 + 800 + 1500 + 200 = 7500 + 1000 = **8500**
I suggest not doing it like that and just ignoring the highlighted zero and then adding it onto the answer. Then you have smaller numbers to work with. Here it is below.

600 + 80 + 150 + 20 = 850 => 8500
You can do this because 340 x 25 is 34 x 10 x 25. You do 34 x 25 and get 850 and then you still need to multiply by ten. You can do that by just adding on the zero.

570 x 42 = 20000 + 2800 + 1000 + 140 = **23940**
           Three zeros added on: two for 500 and one for 40.
           2000 + 280 + 100 + 14 = 2394 => 23940

680 x 91 = **61880**

D.   Multiply.

123 x 45 = 100 x 45 and 20 x 45 and 3 x 45
           = 4500 + 800 + 100 + 120 + 15
           = **5535**

379 x 26 = 300 x 26 and 70 x 26 and 9 x 26
           = 6000 + 1800 + 1400 + 420 + 180 + 54
           = 8000 + 1700 + 154 = **9854**

718 x 32 = 700 x 32 and 10 x 32 and 8 x 32
           = 21000 + 1400 + 320 + 240 + 16
           = **22976**

Day 84
Checking your work

The first will be last. (Matthew 20:24-34)

A.   We're going to do the opposite today. When you do an addition or subtraction problem, you can do the opposite to check your work to see if you were correct.

Here are examples.

35	14		26	39
- 21	+ 21		+ 13	- 13
14	35 ✓		39	26 ✓

Answer these questions and then check your work.

56	**42**		12	**47**		74	**31**
- 14	**+ 14**		+ 35	**- 35**		- 43	**+ 43**
42	**56**		47	**12**		31	**74**

B.   Answer the questions and then do the opposite to check your work.

50	**16**		217	**292**		272	**116**		79	**126**
- 34	**+ 34**		+ 75	**- 75**		- 156	**+ 156**		+ 47	**- 47**
16	**50**		292	**217**		116	**272**		126	**79**

C.   What's the opposite of multiplication? **division** What's the opposite of division? **multiplication**

Do the opposite to check my work.

$225 \div 15 = 15$ $2788 \div 34 = 81$ $735 \div 5 = 149$ $2104 \div 8 = 263$
15 x 15 = 225 ✓   **81 x 34 = 2754 (no)**   **149 x 5 = 745 (no)**   **263 x 8 = 2104** ✓

D.   Answer the question and the do the opposite to check the work.

$305 \div 5 =$ **61** $384 \div 16 =$ **24** $1029 \div 3 =$ **343**

61 x 5 = 305   **16 x 24 = 384**   **343 x 3 = 1029**

Day 85
Review

A. Write one cent plus five cents equals six cents and twenty-five cents and sixty-two cents equals eighty-seven cents. Write them with dollar signs.

$0.01 + $0.05 = $0.06   **$0.25 + $0.62 = $0.87**

Use tally marks to multiply three times seven and five times eight.

21, 40

Add and subtract to check my work.

They are both wrong.

35	**14**	24	**39**
- 22	**+ 22**	+ 13	**- 13**
14	**36**	39	**26**

B. Write one dollar and thirty-one cents plus two dollars and twenty-seven cents equals three dollars and fifty-eight cents.

$1.31 + $2.27 = $3.58

What's 16 times ½?

8

What's 100 x 1, 100 x 0, and 100 x 10?

100, 0, 1000

Check my work. Are my answers correct?

Only the last one is correct.

60	**27**		217	**292**		270	**116**		65	**113**
- 34	**+ 34**		+ 78	**- 78**		- 156	**+ 156**		+ 48	**- 48**
27	**61**		292	**214**		116	**272**		113	**65**

C.   What's $1.00 - $0.40? **$0.60**

What's $1.00 - $0.43? **$0.57**

Subtract. Then check to see if your answers make sense! Add the answer and what you subtracted together.

$1.00	68	$1.00	62	$1.00	33
-$0.32	+ 32	-$0.38	+ 38	-$0.67	+67
$0.68	**100**	**$0.62**	**100**	**$0.33**	**100**

How much would five workers get paid all together if they got paid these different amounts: seven dollars and sixty-five cents, fourteen dollars and forty cents, twenty-six dollars and seventy cents, forty-six dollars and fifteen cents, one hundred and five dollars and sixteen cents.

$200.06

570 x 18 = 57 x 10 and 57 x 8 = 570 + 400 + 56 = 900 + 126 = 1026 => **10,260**

380 x 96 = 38 x 90 and 38 x 6 = 2700 + 720 +180 + 48 = 2000 + 1500 + 148 = 3648 => **36,480**

Do the opposite to check my work.

$2314 \div 9 = 247$
247 x 9 = 2223 (My answer is wrong.)

D.   Add and subtract. Then do the opposite to see if your answers make sense.

$5.00	$1.32	$10.00
-$1.24	+$0.78	- $3.72
$3. 76	**$2.10**	**$6.28**

376 + 124 = 500   **210 – 78 = 132**   **628 + 372 = 1000**

Multiply this amount to find out how much five workers got paid all together.

$15.48

$77.40
You can multiply the dollars by five and the cents by five and then put them together.

638 x 57 = **36,366**

Answer the question and the do the opposite to check the work.

810 ÷ 18 = **45**

18 x 45 = 810

Day 86
Money

They were buying and selling in the temple. (Matthew 21:12-19)

A.   Let's buy low and sell high and figure out our profit. If we bought the toy for five dollars and sold the toy for eight dollars how much profit did we make?

3 dollars

This is how you write that with a dollar sign. $3.00
The amount before the decimal point is the number of dollars. The amount after the decimal point is the number of cents.

Figure out your profit. Buy at $4.00 and sell at $8.00. Buy at twelve dollars and sell at twenty-six dollars. Buy at twenty-one cents and sell at forty-five cents. Buy at $0.35 and sell at $0.79.

$4.00, $14.00, $0.24, $0.49

B.   Find your profit. You can subtract the dollars and cents separately and then combine them.

Buy at $6.35, and sell at $10.50. Buy at $24.23, and sell at $37.45. Buy at $112.03, and sell at $150.22. Buy at $46.18, and sell at $61.25.

C.   What happens when you have negative cents after you subtract? Look at this example. Buy at $1.20, and sell at $3.15. 3 dollars minus 1 dollar is 2 dollars. 15 cents minus 20 cents is minus or negative 5 cents. So the answer is 2 dollars minus 5 cents or $1.95. Or you can write it out like below. These are all the same.

$3.15	315	315	315	315
- $1.20	- 120	-120	-120	-120
2.00	200	205	200	205
-.10	-10	- 10	190	195
+.05	5	195	195	
$1.95	195			

Find your profit. Buy at $15.02, and sell at $23.15. Buy at $13.67, and sell at $46.19. Buy at $53.69, and sell at $80.50. Buy at $23.85, and sell at $30.80.

D.   Find your profit. Buy at $234.20, and sell at $523.00. Buy at $416.36, and sell at $500.00. Buy at $397.62, and sell at $615.50. Buy at $481.68, and sell at $700.00.

Day 87
Weight

A mountain could be thrown into the sea. (Matthew 21:20-27)

A.   We're going to see just how heavy it would be to pick up a mountain. All of the weights I'm using are just made up crazy weights. This isn't a science lesson!

If the mountain weighed nine hundred pounds and eight hundred pounds of people and trees were on top of the mountain, how much would the mountain weigh with everything on top of it? (Hint: Think of it as 9 hundred + 8 hundred.)

9 + 8 = 17, 17 hundred or 1700 pounds

If you had to pick up an anthill mountain and it weighed 8 ounces without the ants and the ants weighed 5 ounces, how much would the anthill weigh with all the ants?

8 + 5 = 13 ounces

What if a termite mound with all the termites weighed 16 pounds and the termites weighed 8 pounds, how much did the termite mound weigh without the termites? If you're not sure how to do it, draw a picture.

8 pounds, 16 – 8 = 8

If you made a mud mountain in your backyard and it was 14 kilograms with the toy cars and trucks you put on top of it that weighed 5 kilograms, how much did the mountain weigh without the cars and trucks on top?

14 – 5 = **9 kilograms**

B.   If the mountain weighed 153 tons and 25 tons of equipment was on the mountain, how much did the mountain weigh with the equipment on top of it?

178 tons

If there was an anthill that weighed 351 grams including the ants, how much did the ants weigh if the anthill alone weighed 327 grams?

24 grams

If there were a termite mound that weighed 209 ounces and the termites weighed 57 ounces, how much did the termite mound weigh when the termites were home?

266 ounces

If you built a mud mountain and it weighed 25 pounds including everything you decorated it with which weighed 8 pounds, how much would the mountain weigh if you took everything off of it?

17 pounds

C. If the mountain weighed eight times as much as the equipment on it and the equipment was 73 tons, how much did the mountain weigh?

584 tons

If the molehill weighed five times as much as the mole that lived it in that weighed 67 ounces, how much does it weigh?

335 ounces

If your mattress/chair/blanket fortress weighs forty-seven times the weight of the pillow being thrown at it, how much does it weigh if the attacking pillow is fifteen ounces.

705 ounces

If the mud mountain weighs 64 times the weight of the toys on it, and the toys are 320 grams, how much does the mud mountain weigh?

320 x 64 = **20,480 grams**

D.   If the toy trucks on the mud hill weighed half of what the mud hill weighed, how much did it weigh if the hill weighed 1528 grams? (Think how you used this fraction to figure out the others.)

764 grams

If the equipment on the mountain weighed one sixth of the mountain, then how much did it weigh if the mountain weighed 468 tons?

78 tons

If the ants on the anthill weighed one twelfth of the anthill, how much did they weigh if the anthill weighed 2592 grams?

 216 grams

If the moles living in the molehill weighed one fifteenth of the molehill, how much did they weigh if the molehill was 675 pounds?

45 pounds

Day 88 (ruler with inches and centimeters - If you don't have inches, just follow the directions and substitute centimeter for inch.)

Length

They dug a wine press. (Matthew 21:28-36)

A. Let's measure how deep the wine press was. Draw a line on the page showing the height of the winepress. Then use a ruler to measure it to the nearest inch. This is like rounding. Is it closest to the 3 or the 4?

   answers will vary

   Then draw lines that are three inches long, five inches long, and seven inches long. Are those numbers all odd or all even?

   odd

B. Now measure the first line you drew to the nearest centimeter.

   answers will vary

   Draw lines that are two centimeters, four centimeters, and eight centimeters long. Are those numbers all odd or even?

   even

C. Now measure the first line you drew to the nearest half inch.

   answers will vary

   Draw lines that are 3.5 inches long, 2.5 inches long, 1.5 inches long.

D. Now measure the line you drew to the nearest tenth of a centimeter. The little lines on your ruler are millimeters. Each millimeter is one tenth of a centimeter. If it measures four lines past the number six on the ruler, then it would measure 7.4 centimeters.

   answers will vary

   Now draw lines that are 1.8 cm, 3.2 cm, 5.5 cm.

Day 89
Weight

The stone became the cornerstone. (Matthew 21:37-46)

A. How would you weigh a heavy cornerstone? A car weighs at least two tons. A baby weighs about 8 pounds. A slice of bread weighs almost one ounce. How would you weigh a heavy stone in tons, pounds, or ounces?

pounds

What measure would you use to weigh a handful of nuts? What measure would you use to weigh a mobile home? What would you use to weigh a book? What about a big box of books?

ounces, tons, ounces, pounds

B. A bag of potatoes weighing a kilogram has about seven potatoes inside. A slice of bread is about 29 grams. Which estimate is best for these items?

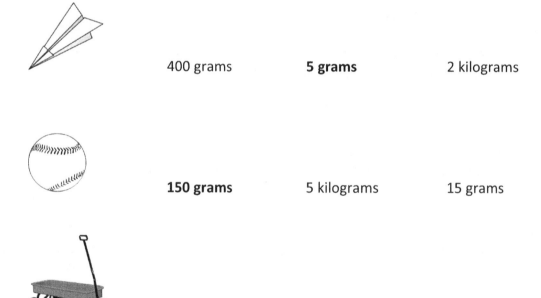

400 grams	**5 grams**	2 kilograms
150 grams	5 kilograms	15 grams
8 kilograms	80 kilograms	800 grams

C.   A gram is one thousandth of a kilogram. A kilogram is one thousand grams. Write these measures as the other.

2000 grams	**2 kilograms**	4 kilograms	**4000 grams**
500 grams	**0.5 kilograms (or ½)**	1.5 kilograms	**1500 grams**

D.   A pound is sixteen ounces. An ounce is one sixteenth of a pound. Write the measures as the other.

128 ounces	**8 pounds**	27 pounds	**432 ounces**
320 ounces	**20 pounds**	139 pounds	**2224 ounces**

Day 90
Review

The apostles were sent out as sheep among wolves. (Matthew 21:12-19)

A.   Figure out your profit. Buy at $14.50, and sell at $7.50. Buy at $3.20, and sell at $8.70.

$7.00, $5.50

If you made a mud mountain in your backyard and it was 14 kilograms with the toy cars and trucks you put on top of it that weighed 6 kilograms, how much did the mountain weigh without the cars and trucks on top?

14 − 6 = **8 kilograms**

Draw lines that are four inches long and two inches long. Are those numbers odd or even?

even

How would you weigh a bus in tons, pounds, or ounces?

tons

What measure would you use to weigh a bag of cotton balls?

ounces

B.   Find your profit. You can subtract the dollars and cents separately and then combine them.

Buy at $16.45, and sell at $37.80. Buy at $128.57, and sell at $150.85.

If the mountain weighed 163 tons and 52 tons of equipment was on the mountain, how much did the mountain weigh with the equipment on top of it?

215 tons

If there was an anthill weighed 431 grams including the ants, how much did the ants weigh if the anthill alone weighed 360 grams?

71 grams

Now measure the line you drew to the nearest centimeter.

answers will vary

Draw lines that are two centimeters, four centimeters, and eight centimeters long. Are those numbers all odd or even?

even

A bag of potatoes weighing a kilogram has about seven inside. A slice of bread is about 29 grams. Which estimate is best for these items?

400 grams   **30 grams**   1 kilogram

4 kilograms   **70 kilograms**   1000 grams

C.   Find your profit. Buy at $15.32, and sell at $64.15. Buy at $27.65, and sell at $48.29.

$48.83, $20.64

If the mountain weighed seven times as much as the equipment on it and the equipment was 143 tons, how much did the mountain weigh?

1001 tons

If your mattress/chair/blanket fortress weighs thirty-eight times the weight of the pillow being thrown at it, how much does it weigh if the attacking pillow is twenty-five ounces.

950 ounces

If the mud mountain weighs 49 times the weight of the toys on it, and the toys are 260 grams, how much does the mud mountain weigh?

260 x 49 = **12,740 grams**

What's 4500 grams in kilograms? **4.5 kilograms**

What's 1.2 kilograms in grams? **1200 grams**

Draw a line that is 2.5 inches long.

D.   Find your profit. Buy at $379.40, and sell at $523.00. Buy at $382.46, and sell at $500.00.

$143.60, $117.54

If the ants on the anthill weighed one twelfth of the anthill, how much did they weigh if the anthill weighed 2016 grams?

168 grams

If the moles living in the molehill weighed one sixteenth of the anthill, how much did they weigh if the molehill was 944 pounds?

59 pounds

Draw a line that is 2.3 cm.

A pound is sixteen ounces. An ounce is one sixteenth of a pound. Write the measures as the other.

176 ounces   **11 pounds**   34 pounds   **544 ounces**

Day 91
Arithmetic

Wedding guests were invited and wedding guests were removed. (Matthew 22:8-14)

A.   We're going to invite and remove wedding guests. If there were 91 wedding guests and 7 more were invited and came, how many would be at the wedding?

16 guests

If there were fifteen guests at the wedding and seven were removed, how many would be left at the wedding?

8 guests

If there were 80 guests and 40 more were invited and came, how many would be in attendance?

120 guests
  80
+ 40
 120 It's really just 8 tens plus 4 tens equals 12 tens.

If there were 130 guests and 60 were removed, how many guests would remain?

70 guests
 130
- 60
  70 It's really just 13 tens minus 6 tens equals 7 tens.

B.   Let's say there are 140 guests. What if 80 were taken away? How many would be left?

60 guests

Now, figure out how many would be left if 10 were taken away, 4, 7, and 13.

130 guests, 136 guests, 133 guests, 127 guests
Check to make sure your answers make sense. If more guests are taken away, there should be fewer guests remaining.

C. If there were 100 guests and 3 were removed, how many would be remaining?

97 guests

How many guests would remain if 30 were removed, 37, 74?

70 guests, 63 guests, 26 guests
Make sure your answers make sense.

What if there were 248 guests at the wedding and five times more were invited and came. How many guests would be at the wedding?

1488 guests

D. Let's say that there were 1000 guests and 8 were removed. How many guests remained?

992 guests

How many guests would remain if 80 were removed, 83, 860, 271?

920 guests, 917 guests, 140 guests, 729 guests
Make sure your answers make sense.

Now let's say there are 1152 guests and they were divided into 16 groups. If one of those groups were removed, how many guests would remain? (Hint: This problem has two parts. It's not asking how many are in each group.)

$1152 \div 16 = 72$ $1152 - 72 = $ **1080 guests**

Groups	Total
	1152
10	- 160
	992
60	- 960
	32
2	- 32
72	0

This isn't the most efficient way, but doing it this way doesn't require you come up with the highest number to multiply by on the first go.

Day 92
Percent

They are to pay their poll tax to Caesar. (Matthew 22:15-22)

A. A percent is a part of a hundred. It's a fraction out of 100 parts. If you drew a circle and divided it into 100 slices and colored in 1 slice, that would be one percent of the circle. If you colored in 38 slices, that would be thirty-eight percent of the circle. Use the example to write the percent amounts.

$^{23}/_{100} = 23\%$ % is the percent sign

$^{37}/_{100} = \mathbf{37\%}$ $^{14}/_{100} = \mathbf{14\%}$

$^{6}/_{100} = \mathbf{6\%}$ $^{75}/_{100} = \mathbf{75\%}$

B. How many cents are in one dollar?

100 cents

What percent of a dollar is one penny? (Hint: How many cents is one penny worth? One. That's one out of one hundred cents in a dollar. This is like the fractions we just did.)   **1%**

What percent of a dollar is one nickel? **5%** (Hint: A nickel is how many cents?)

What percent of a dollar is one dime? **10%**

What percent of a dollar is one quarter? **25%**

C. Write the fraction, the percent, and the money amount in dollars for each of the coin amounts above. Do it for one dollar as well. (Hint: How many cents are in one dollar?)

$1/100 = 1\% = \$0.01$ $10/100 = 10\% = \$0.10$

$5/100 = 5\% = \$0.05$ $25/100 = 25\% = \$0.25$

$100/100 = 100\% = \$1.00$

D. What's 10% of one dollar? What's 10% of ten dollars? (Hint: Ten dollars is ten times one dollar.) What's 10% of one hundred dollars?

$0.10, $1.00, $10.00

Compare the answers. What's the pattern?

The answer is the amount divided by ten.

What's an equivalent fraction of $10/100$ with a denominator of 10? (Hint: How do you get from 100 to 10? You divide by ten. To keep the fraction the same amount, equivalent, you have to divide the top by ten as well.)

$1/10$

To find 10% of something you multiply by one tenth. When you multiply fractions, you are multiplying the top number and dividing the bottom number. Multiplying by one tenth is really just multiplying by one (gives you the same number) and then dividing by ten, so really you are just dividing by ten. When you divide by ten, you are just moving the decimal point over one place.

What's ten percent of $2.40?

$0.24

What percent of one dollar is $5.00? (Hint: Think about what percent of one dollar was one dollar.)

500%

Day 93
Fractions

The Pharisees question Jesus about someone who was married seven times.
(Matthew 22:23-33)

A.   Draw seven stick figure men. Those are the seven husbands. One of those men
      would be one out of her seven husbands. How would you write that as a fraction?

      Here is how you write one out of two as a fraction. ½

      Draw pictures and write the fractions to show these amounts: one third and one
      fifth (one out of three parts and one out of five parts).

      ¹/₇   ¹/₃   ¹/₅

B.   Circle the first husband in the picture you drew. Write that fraction below. Now
      circle another. Write that number, two out of the seven husbands. Circle another
      and write three sevenths. Continue: four sevenths, five sevenths, six sevenths,
      seven seventh.

      ¹/₇   ²/₇   ³/₇   ⁴/₇   ⁵/₇   ⁶/₇   ⁷/₇

C.   Write equations and add and subtract the fractions you wrote above. You could
      draw a picture to show them. Write your answers as a mixed number if the
      numerator (top number) is greater than the denominator (bottom number). Write
      at least four equations. Two should be subtraction and at least one should have a
      mixed number for an answer. Here are an examples.

 $^3/_7 + {}^4/_7 = {}^7/_7 = 1$

 $^7/_7 - {}^2/_7 = {}^5/_7$

D.   Take one of your subtraction equations and one of your addition equations and write them with equivalent fractions. You can look at the previous pictures and draw a line through them to divide each box in half to make them out of fourteen parts. How would that change your numerator and denominator? Your final answer should match your original answer.

Examples using my equations: $6/14 + 8/14 = 14/14 = 1$ $14/14 - 4/14 = 10/14 = 5/7$

Now take your equations and multiply the two numbers instead of adding and subtracting them.

Examples: $7/7 \times 2/7 = 14/49 = 2/7$ $3/7 \times 4/7 = 12/49$

Think, why is the answer to seven sevenths times two sevenths two sevenths? **Because seven sevenths equals one and anything times one is itself.**

Day 94
Testing

The lawyers were testing Jesus. (Matthew 22:34-46)

A.   I'm going to test you today. I'm going to ask you to do your work in your workbook. I'm going to ask you to do something you haven't done before, like maybe use bigger numbers. Can you do it? Yes! So get excited to show your stuff.

1,304	5,975	48,370	39,679	How many legs do five
+ 2,195	- 1,942	+ 20,519	- 12,058	cows have?
3,499	**4,033**	**68,889**	**27,621**	**20**

B.

31,354	75,975	480,240	390,468	How many legs do six
+ 9,195	- 51,348	+ 274,589	- 128,128	chickens and nine cats
40,549	**24,627**	**754,829**	**262,340**	have? **48**

C.   34,526 x 5 = **172,630** (Hint: This is the only one you need to multiply. Break it into parts and use those zeros!)

34,526 x 10 = **345,260**

34,526 x 50 = **1,726,300** (This is x 5 x 10. They already have the answer to x 5, just add a zero to that.)

34,526 x 100 = **3,452,600**

34,526 x 500 = **17,263,000**

34,526 x 1000 = **34,526,000**

34,526 x 5000 = **172,630,000**

34,526 x 5555 = **191,791,930**

(Think! This is 34,526 x 5 and 34,526 x 50 and...)

How would you figure out what's 34,526 x 6666? (Think! Don't multiply.) **The final answer plus the answer to 34,526 x 1000, x 100, x 10, and x 1.**

D. $36 \left(\frac{1}{2}\right) = $ **18** $36 \left(\frac{2}{3}\right) = $ **24**

(36 divided by two times one)

$126 \left(\frac{5}{14}\right) = $ **45** $216 \left(\frac{4}{9}\right) = $ **96**

Day 95
Review

A.   If there were 70 guests at the wedding and 50 more were invited and came, how many would be in attendance at the wedding?

120 guests
  70
+ 50
 120 It's really just 7 tens plus 5 tens equals 12 tens.

If there were 150 guests at the wedding and 80 were removed, how many guests would remain?

70 guests
 150
- 80
  70 It's really just 15 tens minus 8 tens equals 7 tens.

Write the percent amounts.

$7/100 =$ **7%** $94/100 =$ **94%**

Draw pictures and write the fractions to show these amounts: one sixth and one third (one out of six parts and one out of three parts).

$\frac{1}{6}$ $\frac{1}{3}$

   4,502   3,824
+ 2,177   - 1,702
  6,679   **2,122**

How many legs do four cats have?

16 legs

B. Let's say there are 240 guests. What if 80 were taken away? How many would be left?

160 guests

What if instead 8 were taken away?

232 guests

What percent of a dollar is one nickel? **5%**

What percent of a dollar is one quarter? **25%**

What's three sevenths plus one seventh?

⁴/₇

$$\begin{array}{r} 31,354 \\ +\,9,195 \\ \hline \mathbf{40,549} \end{array} \qquad \begin{array}{r} 75,975 \\ -\,51,348 \\ \hline \mathbf{24,627} \end{array}$$

How many legs do seven parrots and four tigers have?

30 legs

C.   If there were 100 guests and 13 were removed, how many would be remaining?

87 guests

How many guests would remain if 78 were removed?

22 guests

What if there were 537 guests at a wedding and five times more were invited and came. How many guests would be at the wedding?

3222 guests
537 x 6 (five times more plus the one there)

Write the fraction, the percent, and the money amount in dollars for each of these amounts: three cents, twelve cents, one dollar.

$^3/_{100}$ = 3% = $0.03 $^{12}/_{100}$ = 12% = $0.12

$^{100}/_{100}$ = 100% = $1.00

Write equations to find the sum and difference of three and twelve cents.

$^3/_{100}$ + $^{12}/_{100}$ = $^{15}/_{100}$ = $^3/_{20}$
You can divide 15 and 100 each by 5 to find an equivalent fraction.

$^{12}/_{100}$ - $^3/_{100}$ = $^9/_{100}$

7,819 x 6 = **46,914**

D.	Let's say that there were 1000 guests and 4 were removed. How many guests remained?

996 guests

How many guests would remain if 347 were removed?

653 guests
Make sure your answers make sense.

Now let's say there are 598 guests and they are divided into 13 groups. If one of those groups were removed, how many guests would remain?

$598 \div 13 = 46$ $598 - 46 =$ **552 guests**

Groups	Total
	598
30	- 390
	208
10	- 130
	78
6	- 78
46	0

What's ten percent of $7.20?

$0.72

What percent of one dollar is $8.00?

800%

$^4/_4 \times {}^2/_9 = {}^8/_{36} = {}^2/_9$ $^3/_7 \times {}^4/_5 = {}^{12}/_{35}$

$192({}^3/_{24}) =$ **24** $322 ({}^4/_7) =$ **184**

Days 96 - 105
Each workbook level has its own problems.

A.

Day 96
Addition: 15, 150
Subtraction: 7, 70
Roman Numerals: 5, 15
Roman Numerals: 2, 13
Decimals: 0.7

Day 97
Addition: 11, 110
Subtraction: 8, 80
Decimals: 0.1, 0.3, 0.5

Day 98
Addition: 15, 150
Subtraction: 8, 80
Numbers: 436, 615
Multiply: 70, 30, 140

Day 99
Addition: 10, 100
Subtraction: 7, 70
Money: $0.1 + $0.10 = $0.11
Money: $0.45 + $0.33 = $0.78
Multiply: 28, 24

Day 100
Check: 33 + 14 = 47 wrong, 67 − 23 = 44 wrong
Add and Subtract: 7,998 ; 1,555
Word problem: 24 legs

A.

Day 101
Add and subtract: 26, 79, 170
Word problem: $4
Fraction: 1/4

Day 102
Add and subtract: 33, 89, 130
Money: $8.00
Money: $4.30
Word problem: 7 kilograms

Day 103
Add and subtract: 13, 186, 90
Measurement: odd
Measurement: tons
Measurement: ounces

Day 104
Add and subtract: 80, 500, 80
Word problem: 120 guests
Word problem: 80 guests
Percent: 9%, 47%
Fraction: 1/7

Day 105
Check: 34 + 45 = 79 wrong, 89 − 36 = 53 wrong
Add and subtract: 7,786 ; 1,164
Word problem: 10 legs

B.

Day 96
Addition: 106, 1060
Addition: 180, 1800
Roman Numerals: 12, 4, 19, 9
Measurement: 3.5 inches

Day 97
Addition: 36, 360
Subtraction: 9, 90
Fractions and decimals: 4/10 0.4, 9/10 0.9
Decimals: 0.1, 0.2, 0.3, 0.4
Fractions: 5/10, 6/10, 7/10, 8/10

Day 98
Addition: 85, 850
Addition: 173, 1730
Numbers: 3264, 7020
Multiply: 150, 100

Day 99
Addition: 13, 130
Subtraction: 49, 490
Negative: 6, 8
Word problem: $219
Fractions:4 3/10, 20 2/3, 150 1/2

Day 100
Check: 57 + 23 = 80 wrong, 564 − 48 = 516 wrong
Check: 216 + 156 = 372 wrong, 101 − 76 = 25 wrong
Add and subtract: 8,467 ; 4,348
Word problem: 32 legs

B.

Day 101
Add and Subtract: $0.04, $0.61
Money: $2.35 + $4.27 = $6.62
Multiply: 6
Multiply: 20, 0, 200

Day 102
Add and subtract: $2.09, $6.94
Word problem: $6.74
Word problem: 160 tons
Word problem: 117 grams

Day 103
Add and subtract: $4.07, $7.55
Measurement: odd
Measurement: 100 kilograms

Day 104
Add and subtract: $7.06, $5.07
Word problem: 240 guests, 312 guests
Percent: 10%
Percent: 1%
Fractions: five eighths

Day 105
Check: 37 + 47 = 84 wrong, 472 − 63 = 409 wrong
Check: 545 + 150 = 695 wrong, 85 − 26 = 59 wrong
Add and subtract: 7,090 ; 4,982
Word problem: 600 legs

C.

Day 96
Arithmetic: 874, $0.53, 2146
Roman numerals: CXXVII, CCCXIX
Measurement: Answers will vary. Example: 10.7 (each millimeter line on the ruler is .1)
Decimals and fractions: 7.2, 7 2/10

Day 97
Arithmetic: 840, $0.38, 4424
Decimals and fractions: 14.7, 3.9, 14 7/10, 3 9/10
Greater than/Less than: <, >

Day 98
Numbers: 23,607 ; 150,114
Multiply: 1734, 2523

Day 99
Word problem: $474
Fractions: 18 2/3
Multiply: 1596
Subtract: 459

Day 100
Subtract: $0.30, $0.27
Subtract: $0.49, $0.82, $0.13
Word problem: $210.06

C.

Day 101
Multiply: 11,310
Multiply: 16, 530
Check: 2536

Day 102
Profit: $60.87
Word problem: 1096 tons
Word problem: 1081 ounces

Day 103
Word problem: 17,020 grams
Multiply: 40,560
Convert: 3.6 kilograms
Convert: 2500 grams
Measurement: 4.25 inches

Day 104
Word problem: 87 guests
Word problem: 22 guests
Word problem: 2685 guests, 3222 guests

Day 105
Fraction and decimal: 17/100, 17%, $0.17, 300/100, 300%, $3.00
Money: $12.25 - $3.12 = $9.13, $12.25 + $3.12 = $15.37
Multiply: 5643

D.

Day 96
Roman numerals: MMCDLI, DCLXXX

Measurement: Answers will vary. Their fractions should be over 16 unless they've been reduced.

Multiply: 17,138

Day 97
Decimals: 0.01, 0.05, 0.10, 0.25

Decimals: 0.48, 471.06

Fractions: 48/100, 471 6/100

Multiply: 25,088

Day 98
Numbers: 429,403

Numbers: 12,674,013

Multiply: 29,944

Negative numbers: $544

Day 99
Arithmetic: 2275, $3.88

Mixed numbers: 30/9 + 10/9 = 40/9 = 4 4/9, 3 1/3 + 1 1/9 = 3 3/9 + 1 1/9 = 4 4/9

Multiply: 11,051

Day 100
Arithmetic: $2.26, $10.43, $5.39

Word problem: $86.95

Divide: 175

D.

Day 101
Multiply: 17,208
Divide: 26, 26 x 18 = 468

Day 102
Money: $226.04
Word problem: 347 grams
Measurement: a line 2.3 centimeters long

Day 103
Word problem: 28 pounds
Measurement: 11 pounds, 464 ounces

Day 104
Word problem: 994 guests
Word problem 817 guests
Word problem: 598 – 46 = 552 guests

Day 105
Percent: $0.61
Percent: 500%
Fractions: 16/72, 8/45
Multiplying fractions: 105, 72

Day 106
Fractions

The gospel of the kingdom will be preached around the world. (Matthew 24:3-14)

A. Draw a circle to be the world. Divide it into four parts. Color in three parts. Let's say that's the part of the world that's heard the gospel of the kingdom. What part of the world is left still needing to hear the gospel?

¼
We write the total number of parts on the bottom. We call that the denominator. The number of parts we're talking about are written on top. We're talking about the one part not colored in, so we write one on top. We call that the numerator.

Write the fraction that shows the part of the world that has already heard the gospel.

³/₄   Three of the four parts of the world

Which is bigger? Use < or > to show it.   **³/₄**   **¹/₄**
> Three of the four parts is more than just one of the four parts.

B. How much of the world is represented by those who have heard the gospel and those who haven't heard the gospel? In other words, add three fourths and one fourth. Look at the circle. There are three colored in. If you added one more quarter and colored it in, how much would be colored in?

All of it, four fourths, one
We say one for the answer. One whole circle is colored in. 3 parts of four plus 1 part of four equals 4 parts of 4 or one whole.

Draw seven circles. Let's say those represent seven countries. How many have heard the gospel so far? None, 0. You could write zero over seven as a fraction, but we never do that. It's just zero, no countries. Now color in each circle one at a time and write the fraction represented by the number of colored-in countries.

¹/₇   ²/₇   ³/₇   ⁴/₇   ⁵/₇   ⁶/₇   ⁷/₇ = 1

What fractions could you add together to get to one? (Hint: Seven sevenths equals one.) Come up with three equations.

$1/7 + 6/7 = 1$ $2/7 + 5/7 = 1$ $3/7 + 4/7 = 1$

C.   Let's start with the whole world and subtract off those who have heard. How many haven't heard the gospel if two fifths have heard? What about if five sixths have heard? What about if five twelfths have heard? What about if seven ninths have heard?

$5/5 - 2/5 = 3/5$ $6/6 - 5/6 = 1/6$

$12/12 - 5/12 = 7/12$ $9/9 - 7/9 = 2/9$

D.   What if three more times had heard than not heard? Then how many would have heard the gospel if two ninths of the world hadn't heard?

$6/9$

Multiply two by three to get six. The number of total parts doesn't change. (Note: This doesn't truly make sense. This leaves eight ninths of the world having either heard or not heard.)

Draw a picture to show six ninths. Figure out an equivalent fraction with a smaller denominator. We call this reducing the fraction. You could use your picture. Make sure to divide the top and bottom number by the same number.

$2/3$

Do it again with four fifteenths having never heard the gospel.

$12/15 \quad = \quad 4/5$

Do it again with five eighteenths having never heard the gospel.

$15/18 \quad = \quad 5/6$

Day 107
Elapsed Time

They are told to flee to the mountains. (Matthew 24:15-22)

A.   First let's practice reading the clock.

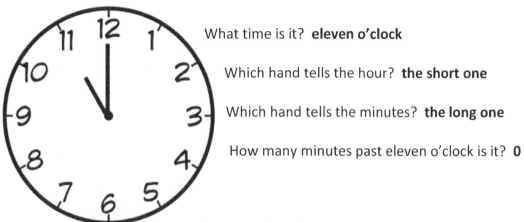

What time is it? **eleven o'clock**

Which hand tells the hour? **the short one**

Which hand tells the minutes? **the long one**

How many minutes past eleven o'clock is it? **0**

Every   time the minute hand gets to a new number, it means five minutes have gone past. Count by fives around the clock to count the minutes.

I'm going to tell you two times. One is when they left. One is when they got to the mountains. You are going to draw the times on the clocks and then figure out how much time has elapsed, how long it took them to get there.

They started at ten in the morning and got there at two in the afternoon. Another group left at 11:00 AM and got there at 6:00 PM.

4 hours   **7 hours**

B.   Now look at this clock. Where is the minute hand? It's gone halfway around. It's half past the hour. Count by fives to figure out how many minutes that is.

30 minutes

What time does the first clock say? **It's eight thirty.**

The minute hand is halfway around, so it's been thirty minutes. Where's the hour hand? It's halfway between 8 and 9. It's halfway past 8. It's 8 and 30 minutes.

Where is the hour hand on this clock? **a little past 3**

How long past three has it been? Count the minutes by five. **15 minutes**

What time is it? **3:15**

Now draw these times and figure how long it took them to flee to the mountains. They started at ten thirty in the morning and got there at two in the afternoon. Another group left at 12:15 PM and got there at 3:30 PM. (Hint: Count on the hours and then count on the minutes to find the second time.)

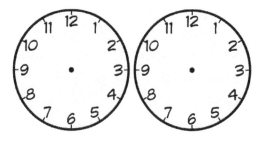

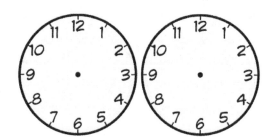

3 ½ hours   **3 hours and 15 minutes**

C.   Draw these times and figure how long it took them to flee to the mountains. They started at seven twenty in the morning and got there at three forty-five that afternoon. Another group left at 9:05 AM and got there at 3:27 PM.

8 hours and 25 minutes   **6 hours and 22 minutes**

D.   Draw these times and figure how long it took them to flee to the mountains. They started at ten thirty-four in the morning and got there at two twelve that afternoon. Another group left at 12:49 PM and got there at 3:14 PM the next day.

3 hours 38 minutes   **26 hours and 25 minutes**

Day 108 (piece of scrap paper)
Geometry

The false prophet will show signs. (Matthew 24:23-31)

A.   Let's look at signs. I'm going to show you shapes, and you tell me what they are and how you know. (Note: You can decide if you want to use the angles in the descriptions. More for older kids, but we have done a lesson on angles, so it can be a little review.)

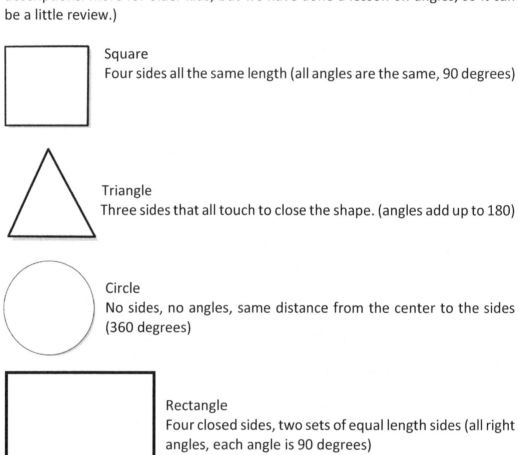

Square
Four sides all the same length (all angles are the same, 90 degrees)

Triangle
Three sides that all touch to close the shape. (angles add up to 180)

Circle
No sides, no angles, same distance from the center to the sides (360 degrees)

Rectangle
Four closed sides, two sets of equal length sides (all right angles, each angle is 90 degrees)

B.   Identify the three dimensional shapes and tell how you know what shape it is. Describe it.

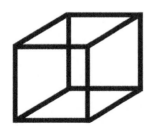

Cube
Six equal square sides

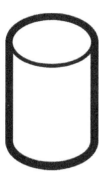

Cylinder
Equal sized circles on top and bottom, rectangular side wrapped around (Just roll up a piece of paper to see that a rectangle makes a cylinder)

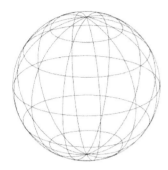

Sphere
ball shaped, equal distance from the center to the side in every direction

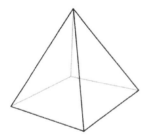

Pyramid
Straight side base, triangle sides that meet at a point

C.   What's a congruent shape? **a shape of the same size and shape** Identify the shapes and describe how to identify that shape. They are all polygons. A polygon is a flat, closed figure with straight sides.

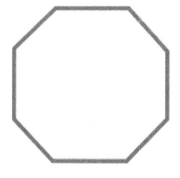

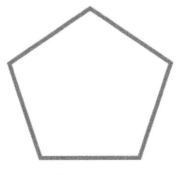

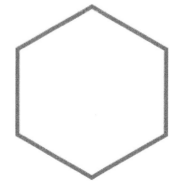

Octagon
eight-sided polygon

Pentagon
five-sided polygon

Hexagon
six-sided polygon

D.   Identify the polygons. Describe them.

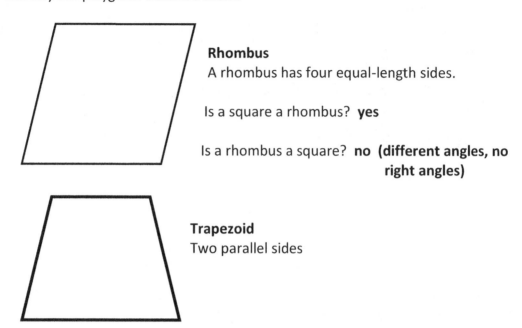

Rhombus
A rhombus has four equal-length sides.

Is a square a rhombus? **yes**

Is a rhombus a square? **no (different angles, no right angles)**

Trapezoid
Two parallel sides

Parallel lines go the same exact direction. The top and bottom of a square or rectangle are parallel lines. The two sides are parallel to each other. In the word parallel there are two Ls next to each other that look like parallel lines. How many sets of parallel lines are in a parallelogram (shown below)? **2**

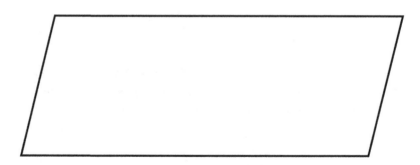

Day 109
Fractions

Two would be in the field and one would be taken. (Matthew 24:32-41)

A.   If two people were in the field and one was taken, what fraction of the people were taken? Draw two people. Circle one of them. Write the fraction showing how many people were taken.

½

What does the numerator, the top number show? **how many were taken**

What does the denominator, the bottom number, show? **how many people are there total**

Add three more people to your drawing. Circle two of them to show that two people were taken. How do you think you would show the fraction of how many people were taken?

$2/5$ **two out of the five people**

Add two more people to your drawing and circle two more. Write the new fraction.

$4/7$ **four out of the seven people**

B.   If two fifths were taken and then three fifths were taken, how many were taken all together? Draw a picture to show two fifths. Draw five people and circle two of them. Then circle three more. Write the equation with the answer.

$2/5$ + $3/5$ = $5/5$ = 1 **Five out five people is all of them, one whole group, not a fraction of the group**

Write another fractional equation that equals one.

Answers will vary. The denominators should all be the same. The numerators added together should equal the denominator.

C.	If you have seven people and three are taken, write an equation with the answer to show what faction of the group are left behind.

$^7/_7$ - $^3/_7$ = $^4/_7$

Write another fraction equation showing how many were left behind.

Answers will vary. The denominators should all be the same. The numerators in the answer and in the number being subtracted should add up to the first numerator.

D.	If three times more people were taken then were left behind, how many were left behind if 24 were taken? Answer the question and then write it as a fraction. Reduce the fraction. (Hint: Three times the number of people left behind equals twenty-four.)

8 people $24 \div 3 = 8$
8 + 24 = 32 people total
$^8/_{32}$ = $^1/_4$ $8 \div 8 = 1$ $32 \div 8 = 4$ This is reducing the fraction by finding an equivalent fraction. If you aren't sure, you can at least see that they are both even numbers (8 and 32), so you can divide both by two to get started. (4 and 16 are also both even, so you could divide by two or maybe you'd notice they can both be divided by four.)

Do it again. If four times the number of people were taken as were left behind, how many were left behind if 20 were taken? Answer the question and then write it as a fraction.

5 people $20 \div 4 = 5$
5 + 20 = 25 people total
$^5/_{25}$ = $^1/_5$ $5 \div 5 = 1$ $25 \div 5 = 5$

A.   Draw a picture that shows three parts. Color in two. Write a fraction that shows
        how many are colored in and how many are not colored in. Use a greater than/less
        than symbol to show which is bigger.

2/3   >   1/3

Two of the three parts is more than just one of the three parts.

A group started at eleven in the morning and got there at four in the afternoon.
Another group left at 7:00 AM and got there at 3:00 PM. How long did it take them
to get there?

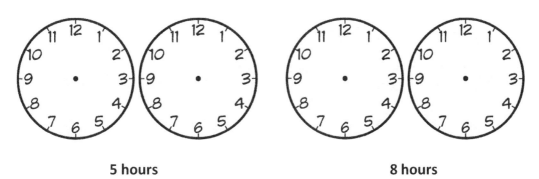

5 hours   **8 hours**

Name the shapes.

Has four sides all the same length _____

Has four sides with two sets of equal-length sides _____

Has three sides that all touch _____

Has no straight sides _____

Square, rectangle, triangle, circle

If five people were in the field and one was taken, what fraction of the people
were taken? What fraction were left behind? Which is greater?

1/5 < 4/5

B.   Write a fraction addition equation that adds up to 1. Write a fraction subtraction equation. (That means it includes the answer!)

Answers will vary. See Days 106 and 109.

What time is it?

9:45

Draw these times and figure how long it took them to flee to the mountains. They started at six thirty in the morning and got there at one in the afternoon.
Another group left at 1:15 PM and got there at 4:45 PM.

6 ½ hours   **3 hours and 30 minutes**

Name the shapes.

Made from two circles and a rectangle _____**cylinder**

Made from a straight-side base and triangles that meet at a point._____ **pyramid**

Made with six equal squares _____**cube**

Made with no straight sides. Every point on it is the same distance from its

center. _____ **sphere**

C.	How many haven't heard the gospel if three fifths have heard? What about if four ninths have heard?

$^5/_5$ - $^3/_5$ = $^2/_5$ $^9/_9$ - $^4/_9$ = $^5/_9$

Draw these times and figure how long it took them to flee to the mountains. They started at seven ten in the morning and got there at two fifty that afternoon. Another group left at 8:25 AM and got there at 3:57 PM.

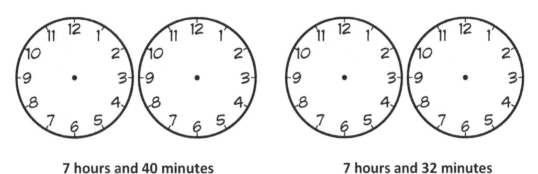

7 hours and 40 minutes   **7 hours and 32 minutes**

Which of these is a polygon?

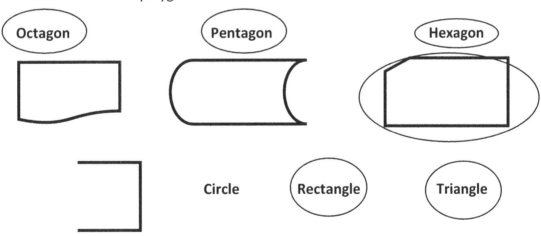

D.   What if four more times had heard than not heard? Then how many would have heard the gospel if two twelfths of the world hadn't heard? Reduce the fraction.

⁸/₁₂   =   ²/₃

If four times the number of people were taken as were left behind, how many were left behind if 28 were taken? Answer the question and then write it as a fraction.

7 people   28 ÷ 4 = 7
7 + 28 = 35 people total
⁷/₃₅ = ¹/₅   7 ÷ 7 = 1 35 ÷ 7 = 5

Draw these times and figure how long it took them to flee to the mountains. They started at six fourteen in the morning and got there at one seven that afternoon. Another group left at 2:39 AM and got there at 4:04 PM the next day.

6 hours 53 minutes   **37 hours and 25 minutes**

Identify how many sets of parallel lines are in the shapes.

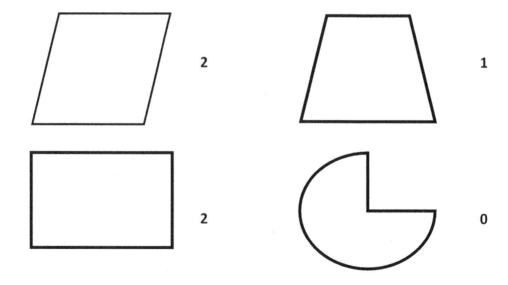

2

1

2

0

Day 111
Fractions, liquid measurements

The foolish women asked for oil for their lamps. (Matthew 25:1-13)

A.   Let's learn about the measurements of liquids. Outside of America most liquids
      are measured in liters. One liter is 1000 milliliters.

      How many milliliters is two liters of oil?

      2000 ml (millimeters)

      How many liters of oil is 5000 milliliters of oil?

      5 l (liters)

      How many milliliters is half a liter? (Hint: 5 + 5 = 10, 50 + 50 = 100)

      500 ml

B.   Cut out the pieces in your workbook and figure out the following:
      (I included the pieces in this book too, but not for cutting. They can also be printed
      from our site if you don't want to cut your workbook.)

      How many cups are in a pint? **2**

      How many pints are in one quart? **2**

      How many quarts are in a gallon? **4**

C.   Use what you know. How many pints are in a gallon? **8**

      How many cups are in a quart? **4**

      How many cups are in a gallon? **16**

D.   Use what you know. What part of a gallon is a cup? $^1/_{16}$

A pint? $^1/_8$ A quart? ¼ (as a decimal, 0.25, 25%)

What part of a quart is a pint? ½

Can you write that as a decimal? **0.5**

Can you write that as a percent? **50%**

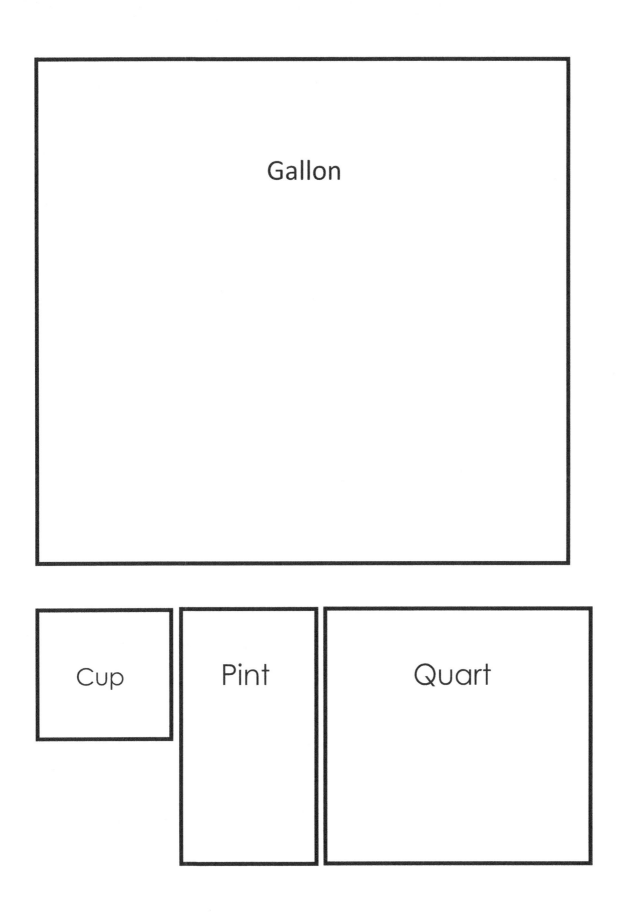

Day 112
Word Problems (arithmetic, negative numbers)

A man was given five talents and received back five more. (Matthew 25:14-23)

A. If a man was given five talents and went to work with it and got back double, how many talents did he have in the end?

10 talents

If a man was given twelve talents and went to work with it and got back double, how many talents did he have in the end?

24 talents

If a man was given forty-three talents and went to work with it and got back double, how many talents did he have in the end?

86 talents

Let's say the slave was given eight talents and in the end just had five to give back to his master. What happened?

8 talents _____ = 5 talents

He lost three talents. - 3, negative three or minus 3, 8 – 3 = 5

B. If a man ended up with twenty-four talents and had started with seven, how many talents did he earn with his investment?

17 talents

If a man ended up with one hundred thirteen talents and had started with seventy-six, how many talents did he earn with his investment?

37 talents

If a man ended up with two hundred twenty-two talents and had started with one hundred five, how many talents did he earn with his investment?

117 talents

If a slave started with ten talents and ended with four talents, how many talents did he "earn?"

- 6 talents

C.   If the slave earned five times the amount of the original investment, how much did she earn if she had been given 27 talents?

135 talents

If the slave earned twenty-four times the amount of the original investment, how much did she earn if she had been given 39 talents?

936 talents

If the slave earned eight times the amount of the original investment, how much did she earn if she had been given 356 talents?

2848 talents

If a slave started with one hundred talents and ended with forty-six talents, how many talents did he "earn?"

- 54 talents

D.   If the slave earned a fifth of his original investment, how much did he earn if he was originally given 275 talents?

55 talents

If the slave earned a sixteenth of his original investment, how much did he earn if he was originally given 224 talents?

14 talents

If the slave earned a seventh of his original investment, how much did he earn if he was originally given 217 talents?

31 talents

If a slave started with one thousand five hundred talents and ended with seven hundred sixty-eight talents, how many talents did he "earn?"

- 732 talents

Day 113
Decimals

The bank would pay interest on the money. (Matthew 25:24-30)

A.   We're going to invest our money and get back interest. We're going to invest at 10%. That's an easy numbers to figure things out for.

Let's say you have ten dollars to invest. Write down ten.

Now let's say you invest it at ten percent. That means you earn a dollar from your investment. Look at the number ten. Can you draw a decimal point to turn it into a 1?

1.0
There is one digit after the decimal point.

Now figure out how much money you would earn from your investment of twenty dollars, fifty dollars, and eighty dollars.

$2, $5, $8

B.   Now let's invest at just 1 percent. That means you earn ten cents from your money. Write the number ten again. Can you draw in a decimal point to make it say ten cents? (Hint: $1.50 is one dollar and fifty cents.)

.10
There are two digits after the decimal point.

Now figure out how much money you would earn from your investment of twenty dollars, fifty dollars, and eighty dollars.

$0.20, $0.50, $0.80

C. Write the number ten one more time. This time place a decimal point but make it say ten dollars.

$10.00

There's basically an invisible decimal point after all whole numbers. The number 5 can also be written 5.000000000000, but that's inconvenient. We like to keep things as easy as we can. Those zeros don't change the value at all, so we just leave them off.

When we are finding ten percent and one percent we are really just moving the decimal point. In both cases there is a one in the number. What happens to numbers when you multiply them by one? **They stay the same.** What happens when you multiply by ten? **You are multiplying by one. Then you just add on the zero.**

Write $10.00 x 10 = $100.00 and watch what happens to the decimal point?

It moves over one to the right.

To find ten percent we just move the decimal point the other way, to the left. The numbers are going to get smaller. A percent is a part of a whole, like a fraction.

What's ten percent of $100? $10
What's ten percent of $10? $1
What's ten percent of $1 $0.10
What's ten percent of $0.10 $0.01

Figure out how much money you would have after your investment of seven dollars and two hundred dollars. Figure out the total amount of money you would have after you earned ten percent on your investment and then again with earning one percent on your investment. (Hint: How would you write seven cents and 100 cents? 0.07 and 1.00.)

7 dollars at 10% = 0.7 **$7.70**
7 dollars at 1% = .07 **$7.07**

200 dollars at 10% = 20.0 **$220**
200 dollars at 1% = 2.00 **$202**

Now find the difference between what you earned at ten and one percent.

$0.63, $18

D. When you are finding ten percent, you are multiplying by point one (.1). When you multiply by one, what happens? **The number stays the same**. So the only thing that is really changing is the decimal point.

What do you think you multiply by to find one percent?

.01

The one means the number stays the same and the decimal point shows us there has to be two decimal places in the answer, two numbers after the decimal point. We just take the number and move the decimal point over two times.

To find 20% we just find the answer to ten percent and then multiply by two. To find 5% we just find one percent by moving the decimal point and then multiply by five. Or, you could multiply by five and then move the decimal point. Or, you could find ten percent and then divide in half. Whichever you find easier!

Find 1, 5, 10, 15, 20, and 25 percent of $10.00.

$10.00 → **$0.10, $0.50, $1.00, $1.50, $2.00, $2.50**

How would you find 34% of $10?

Multiply the answer for 10% by 3 and 1% by 4.

Day 114
Roman Numerals

In our lesson today we learn about Louis XIV. (Matthew 25:31-40)

A.   We're going to read and write Roman Numerals today. Do you remember how to write 1, 5, or 10?

I, V, X

How do you think you would write 15?

XV
The biggest number goes on the left. Then you add on what comes after it.

Figure out what these numbers are:

VIII = **8**   XX = **20**   XVII = **17**   XI = **11**

B.   What does it mean when a smaller number comes before a bigger number as in IV?

That is four. You subtract off the smaller number when it comes before the bigger number.

XI is eleven. What's IX?

9
You only do that will fours and nines.

Figure out these numbers:

IX = **9**   XXIV = **24**   XIII = **13**   XXXVI = **36**

C.   Do you remember what letters represent 50 and 100?

L and C

How would you write 253?

CCLIII
You write each place value in order, left to right, one at a time, 200, 50, 3.

How would you write 175, 196, and 284?

CLXXV, CXCVI, CCLXXXIV

D.   Do you remember how to write 500 and 1000?

D and M

What would be 1769 in Roman numerals?

MDCCLXIX

How would you write these numbers?

1092, 484, 999, 3149

MXCII, CDLXXXIV, CMXCIX, MMMCXLIX
You can't write IM for 999. You have to write out each place value: 900, 90, 9.

Day 115
Review

A.   How many millimeters is a liter and a half? (Hint: How many millimeters are in one liter and how many are in half a liter?)

1500 ml

If a man was given thirty-two talents and went to work with it and got back double, how many talents did he have in the end?

64 talents

Let's say the slave was given twelve talents and in the end just had five to give back to his master. What happened?

Lost seven talents

Figure out how much money you would earn from your investment of twenty dollars, fifty dollars, and eighty dollars if you earned ten percent interest.

$2, $5, $8

Figure out what these numbers are:

IX = **9**   XXII = **22**   XXV = **25**   XVI = **16**

B.   There are two cups are in a pint. There are two pints in a quart. How many cups are in a quart? Draw a picture to help you.

4 cups

If a man ended up with three hundred eighty-one talents and had started with two hundred thirty-five, how many talents did he earn with his investment?

146 talents

If a slave started with fifteen talents and ended with eight talents, how many talents did he "earn?"

- 7 talents

Figure out how much money you would have after your investment of 40 dollars. Figure out the total amount of money you would have after you earned ten percent and one percent on your investment. (Hint: How would you write seven cents and 100 cents? 0.07 and 1.00.)

40 dollars at 10% = 4 **$44.00**
40 dollars at 1% = 0.4 **$40.40**

Figure out these numbers:

XV = **15**   XIV = **14**   XIX = **19**   XXVII = **27**

C.   There are 8 pints in a gallon. There are 4 cups in a quart.

How many cups are in a gallon?

16 cups

If the slave earned six times the amount of the original investment, how much did she earn if she had been given 297 talents?

1782 talents

If a slave started with one hundred talents and ended with thirty-one talents, how many talents did he "earn?"

- 69 talents

Figure out how much money you would have after your investment of 6 dollars and three hundred dollars. Figure out the total amount of money you would have after you earned ten percent and one percent on your investment. (Hint: How would you write seven cents and 100 cents? 0.07 and 1.00.)

6 dollars at 10% = 0.6 **$6.60**
6 dollars at 1% = 0.06 **$6.06**

300 dollars at 10% = 30 **$330.00**
300 dollars at 1% = 3   **$303.00**

Now find the difference between what you earned at ten and one percent.

$5.40, $27.00

How would you write 93, 394, and 178?

XCIII, CCCXCIV, CLXXVIII

D. There are sixteen cups in a gallon. What fraction shows how many cups in a half gallon? What fraction of a half gallon is one cup?

$^8/_{16} = ^1/_2$

$^1/_8$

There are two cups in a pint. What percentage of a pint is a cup?

50%

If the slave earned a sixth of his original investment, how much did he earn if he was originally given 318 talents?

53 talents

If a slave started with two thousand three hundred talents and ended with one thousand one hundred twenty-six talents, how many talents did he "earn?"

- 1174 talents

Find 1, 5, 10, 15, 20, and 25 percent of $27.00.

$27.00 → **$0.27, $1.35, $2.70, $4.05, $5.40, $6.75**

How would you write these numbers?

1931, 2759

MCMXXXI, MMDCCLIX

Day 116

Money

She poured out costly perfume on Jesus' feet. (Matthew 26:6-16)

A.   Let's talk about how expensive that perfume was.

Write an amount of money with a bunch of zeros. Make sure to use a dollar sign and decimal point.

Now double that amount.

Now double that amount.

Now double that amount.

The number of zeros will stay the same.

B.   When you add or subtract money, you can do it just like a regular number. You can ignore the decimal point, but you have to make sure it is in your answer.

To add $4.95 and $6.25 You would add 4 dollars and 6 dollars, 90 cents and 20 cents, and 5 cents and 5 cents. That's 10 dollars, 110 cents, and 10 cents. $10 + 120 cents = $10 + $1.20 = $11.20

Here's a subtraction example.

$3.15	315
- $1.20	- 120
2.00	200
-.10	-10
+.05	5
$1.95	195 -> $1.95

Money will always have two digits after the decimal point.

Let's say the perfume is usually priced $42.95, but today it's on sale for just $15.80. How much could you save if you bought it today?

$27.15
Subtract.

You buy the perfume for $42.95 and a nice card for $3.76. How much did you spend?

$46.71
Add.

Let's say the perfume is usually priced $62.05, but today it's on sale for just $23.80. How much could you save if you bought it today?

$38.25
Subtract.

You buy the perfume for $78.50 and a nice card for $4.67. How much did you spend?

$83.17
Add.

C.   Let's say the perfume is ten times more expensive than the watch that costs $35.17. How much does the perfume cost? First, what is ten times 3? **30** What is ten times 35? **350** What is ten times 351? **3,510** What is ten times 3517? **35,170**

What do you think is $35.17 times ten if 3517 times ten is 35,170?

$351.70
There are always two decimal places in money, two digits after the decimal point.

Now multiply $35.17 by 100. First think, what's 3517 times 100?

$3517.00

Multiply these amounts by ten and one hundred: $2.05, $14.67, $243.99

$20.50 and $205.00, $146.70 and $1,467.00, $2,439.90 and $24,399.00

D. To multiply by ten you move the decimal point one to the right. To divide by ten you move the decimal point one to the left. Together look at the last answers. Divide by ten and divide by ten again to get the "multiply by ten" answers and then the original numbers.

How do you think you could multiply 0.5 by ten?

5
Decimal point goes one to the right. 5 times 10 is 50. .5 x 10 has one decimal place in the question, so there is one decimal place in the answer, 5.0 . We just write 5 because it's easier.

How do you think you would divide 7 by ten?

0.7
The decimal point moves one to the left. Where waws it? You could write seven as 7.000000000000000 and it would still be seven. We just don't waste our time and write a decimal point when it's not necessary.

Multiply and divide by ten over and over. Place your answer on the next line.

10 x 13.452 =
10 x
10 x
10 x
10 x

134.52   ÷ 10 =
            ÷ 10 =
            ÷ 10 =
            ÷ 10 =
            ÷ 10 =

Multiply: **134.52; 1,345.2; 13,452; 134,520; 1,345,200**
Have them read the numbers to you.
one hundred thirty-four and fifty-two hundredths, one thousand three hundred forty-five and two tenths, thirteen thousand four hundred and fifty-two, one hundred thirty-four thousand five hundred twenty, one million three hundred forty-five thousand two hundred.

Divide: **13.452, 1.3452, .13452, 0.013452, 0.0013452**
You don't have to read all of these. The first is 13 and 452 thousandths.

Day 117
Scale Maps

Jesus sent the disciples into the city. (Matthew 26:17-25)

You are going to draw a map. Mark one place on the page, "You are here." Mark another place on the page with the donkey they need to get to.

Draw streets to get from here to there.

Decide how far each centimeter or inch on your drawing is in miles or kilometers.

Measure the distance along the roads you would need to travel to get to the donkey.

Multiply that amount by the distance represented by each measurement.

How far do you need to travel to get the donkey?

Day 118
Multiplication and Division Word Problems

The rooster crowed three times. (Matthew 26:26-35)

A. Let's do things three times. If you sold six bags of cookies to each of three customers, how many bags of cookies did you sell all together?

6 + 6 + 6 = **18 bags of cookies**

What if you sold three bags of cookies to each of six customers, how many bags would you have sold all together?

3 + 3 + 3 + 3 + 3 + 3 = **18 bags of cookies**
It's the same amount. It doesn't matter if you add 6 three times or 3 six times.

What if you received two votes from three different families for best snowman, how many votes did you receive all together?

2 + 2 + 2 = **6 votes**
Two three times is six. Two times three is six.

How many votes did you receive if you received 3 votes from two different families?

3 + 3 = **6 votes**
Three two times is six. Three times two is six.

If you sold twelve bags of cookies to each of three customers, how many bags of cookies did you sell all together?

12 + 12 + 12 = **36 bags of cookies**

What if you sold three bags of cookies to each of twelve customers, how many bags would you have sold all together?

36 bags of cookies
It's the same amount.

What if you received twenty-one votes from three different families for best snowman, how many votes did you receive all together?

21 + 21 + 21 = **63 votes**

How many votes did you receive if you received 3 votes from twenty-one different families?

63 votes

B.   Now we're going to do the opposite. If you sold twelve bags of cookies in total to three people, how many bags of cookies did you sell to each person if they each bought the same number of bags? How would you figure that out?

You could draw a picture of twelve bags and divide them into three even groups.

* * * * | * * * * | * * * *

You are going to divide twelve by three. To multiply we added the numbers over and over again. To divide we can do the opposite and subtract numbers over and over again. Subtract three over and over from twelve until you don't have any left. How many times did you subtract 3?

4
They each bought 4 bags of cookies.

If you sold twenty bags of cookies in total to four people, how many bags of cookies did you sell to each person if they each bought the same number of bags?

5 people
Divide 20 into 4 groups of 5 or subtract four from twenty five times.

Let's say you got forty votes from ten families. Divide to find out about how many people voted from each family.

4 people

C.   If you sold sixty-four bags of cookies to each of three customers, how many bags of cookies did you sell all together?

64 x 3 = **192 bags of cookies**

What if you received twenty-seven votes from three different families for best snowman, how many votes did you receive all together?

27 x 3 = **81 votes**

If you sold three bags of cookies to each of one hundred fifty-eight customers, how many bags of cookies did you sell?

3 x 158 = 300 + 150 + 24 = **474 bags of cookies**

What if you received three votes from two hundred thirty-six voters for best snowman (for most creative, best design, highest quality construction), how many votes did you receive?

236 x 3 = 600 + 90 + 18 = **708 votes**

D.   If you divided two hundred seven cookies into bags of nine cookies each, how many bags of cookies could you make?

23 bags
Divide 207 into groups of 9.

```
 9 | 207          9 | 207
10 | -90         20 |-180
   | 117            |  27
10 | -90          3 | - 27
   |  27         23 |   0
 3 | - 27
23 |   0
```

If you divided three hundred seventy-eight cookies evenly into bags of fourteen cookies each, how many bags did you need?

27 cookies
Divide 378 into groups of 14.

```
14 | 378         14 | 378
10 |-140         20 | -280
   | 238            |  98
10 |-140          7 | -98
   |  98         27 |   0
 2 | -28
   |  70
 4 | -56
   |  14
 1 | - 14
27 |   0
```

If you divided one hundred twenty-three cookies into bags of six cookies each, how many cookies are left over without a bag?

3 cookies 3 is called the remainder. It's what remains.
Divide 123 into 6 groups.

6	123
10	-60
	63
10	-60
	3

6	123
20	-120
	3

If you divided two hundred seventy-nine cookies into bags of fifteen cookies each, how many cookies are left over without a bag?

9 cookies
Divide 123 into 6 groups.

15	279
10	-150
	129
2	-30
	99
4	- 60
	39
2	- 30
	9

15	279
10	-150
	129
8	-120
	9

Day 119
Time

The disciples couldn't stay awake for one hour. (Matthew 26:36-41)

A. First let's practice reading the clock. Which hand is the hour hand? **short** Which hand is the minute hand? **long** Which number has the hour hand last passed? **8** That's the hour. It's eight something. It's not eight o'clock exactly because the minute hand isn't pointing straight up to the twelve. Each number on the clock represents five minutes. Count by fives around the clock and stop at the six, where the minute hand is pointing. How many minutes past eight is it? **thirty minutes** What time is it? **eight thirty**

I'm going to tell you two times. One is when the disciples fell asleep. The other is when they woke up. You are going to draw the times on the clocks and then figure out how long they slept.

They fell asleep at ten in the morning woke up at ten thirty. Then they fell back asleep at 11:00 PM and woke up at 11:30 PM.

30 minutes   **30 minutes**

B.　Now look at this clock. Where is the minute hand? **It's at the 2.** Count by fives to figure out how many minutes that is.

10 minutes

What time does the clock say? **It's four ten.**

Now draw these times and figure how long the disciples slept. They fell asleep at nine in the evening and got woken up at ten thirty-five. Then they fell back asleep at 11:15 PM and woke up at 11:40 PM.

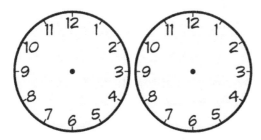　　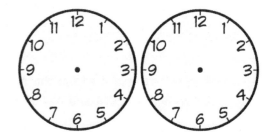

one hour and thirty-five minutes　　　　**25 minutes**

C.　Draw these times and figure how long they slept. They fell asleep at eight twenty at night and were woken up at ten forty. Then they fell back asleep at 10:55 PM and woke up again at 11:25.

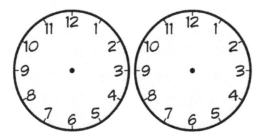　　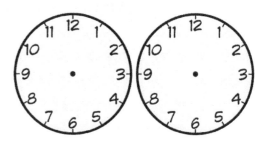

2 hours and 20 minutes　　　　**30 minutes**

D. Draw these times and figure how long the disciples slept. They fell asleep at nine twenty-four in the evening and woke up at eleven twelve. Then they fell back asleep at 11:43 PM and stayed asleep until 7:27 AM the next morning.

1 hours 48 minutes   **7 hours and 44 minutes**

Day 120
Review

A.   Write twenty-three dollars and thirty cents. Can you double that amount?

$23.30, $46.60

Draw a line that's four centimeters long and write how far that would be if it were on a map and each centimeter represents 100 miles.

400 miles

If you sold five bags of cookies to each of seven customers, how many bags of cookies did you sell?

5 + 5 + 5 + 5 + 5 + 5 + 5 = **35 bags of cookies**

What if you received six votes from five different families for best snowman, how many votes did you receive?

5 + 5 + 5 + 5 + 5 + 5 = **30 votes**
They can count by fives. They don't have to add six five times. Five six times is the same amount.

What time is it? **four thirty**

They fell asleep at 9:00 PM and woke up at 9:30 PM. How long did they sleep?

30 minutes

B.   The perfume is usually priced $56.20 but today it's on sale for just $34.05. How much could you save?

$22.15
Subtract.

You buy the perfume for $37.85 and a nice card for $4.65. How much did you spend?

$42.50
Add.

Draw a line that's three inches long and write how far that would be if it were on a map and each inch represents 300 miles.

If you sold twenty-four bags of cookies to four people, how many bags of cookies did you sell to each person if they each bought the same amount?

6 bags
Divide 24 into 4 groups of 6 or subtract four from twenty-four six times.

Let's say you got forty votes from five families. Divide to find out about how many people voted from each family.

8 people

What time does the first clock say? **It's seven forty.**

The disciples fell asleep at 10:25 PM and woke up at 11:30 PM. Draw the times and find how long they were asleep.

one hour and five minutes

C. Let's say the perfume is ten times more expensive than the watch that costs $28.97. How much does the perfume cost?

$289.70

If the perfume cost 100 times the cost of the notebook at $1.23, how much does the perfume cost?

$123.00

Draw a line that's eight centimeters long and write how far that would be if that distance were on a map where each centimeter represents 150 miles.

1200 miles

If you sold seven bags of cookies to each of two hundred thirty-nine customers, how many bags of cookies did you sell?

7 x 239 = **1673 bags of cookies**

Draw these times and figure how long the disciples slept. They fell asleep at 9:35 PM and woke up at 11:10.

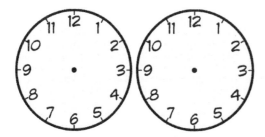

1 hour and 35 minutes

D. Multiply and divide by ten over and over. Place your answer on the next line.

10 x 21.379 =

10 x

10 x

10 x

10 x

527.84   ÷ 10 =

            ÷ 10 =

            ÷ 10 =

            ÷ 10 =

            ÷ 10 =

Multiply: **213.79, 2137.9; 21,379; 213,790; 2,137,900**
Divide: **52.784, 5.2784, 0.52784, 0.052784, 0.0052784**

Draw a line that's six centimeters long and write how far that would be if it were on a map where each centimeter represents 150 miles.

900 miles

If you divided six hundred and twelve cookies evenly into bags of seventeen cookies each, how many bags did you need?

36 cookies
Divide 612 into groups of 17.

```
17 | 612          17 | 612
10 |-170          30 |-510
     442               102
20 |-340           6 |-102
     102          36|   0
 1 | -17
      85
 4 | - 68
      17
 1 | - 17
36|   0
```

If you sold twenty-eight bags of cookies to each of thirty-six customers, how many bags of cookies did you sell?

28 x 36 = **1008 bags of cookies**

Draw these times and figure how long the disciples slept. They fell asleep at 9:31 PM and stayed asleep until 5:12 AM the next morning.

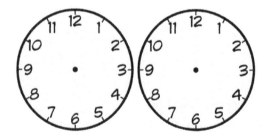

7 hours 41 minutes

Day 121 (It would be nice to have a block on hand.)
Surface Area

Peter went into the courtyard. (Matthew 26:51-58)

A.   In our science lesson today we use the term surface area. I want to find different surface areas today. Do you remember what area is? It's how big a flat surface is, how much area it covers.

If the courtyard were five yards long and ten yards wide, what would its area be? (Hint: That's like laying blocks down in five rows of ten. Another hint: You could count by ten to count up how many blocks were in all those rows together.)

50 square yards

That would be the area of the courtyard.

If you wanted to paint a whole room, floor, walls, and ceiling, you'd have to find out how much surface area you'd need to cover with paint, so you'd buy enough. What would you need to know to find the surface area of the whole room?

the area of each wall, the floor, and the ceiling, so you'd need to know the length and width of each one

Let's say there was a room that was the shape of a perfect cube. What would that look like? How many sides would it have? You could get out a block to count.

like a square block, or like dice, 6 sides

In a perfect cube each of the six sides is a square. If each side had an area of 5 meters squared, what would be the total surface area of the cube? (Hint: They could count by five for the six sides.)

30 meters squared

B.   Find the surface area of a cube where each side is a square with a length of ten centimeters. First find the surface area of one side.

600 cm^2, centimeters squared
10 x 10 = 100 cm^2, area for each side, then six times

What would be the surface area of a cube where each side had a length of five inches?

150 in²
5 x 5 = 25 (one side), six times

C.   What would be the surface area of a cube where each side had a length of twenty-three centimeters?

3174 cm²
23 x 23 = 529 (one side), six times

What would be the surface area of a cube where each side had a length of eighteen inches?

1944 in²
18 x 18 = 324 (one side), six times

What would be the surface area of a cube where each side had a length of twenty-five centimeters?

3750 cm²
25 x 25 = 625 (one side), six times

D.   What would be the surface area of a cube where each side had a length of sixty-eight inches?

27,744 in²
68 x 68 = 4624 (one side), six times

If the surface area of a cube were 384 in², what is the length of one side?

8 in.
384 divided by 6 = 64   8 x 8 = 64

If the surface area of a cube were 726 cm², what is the length of one side?

11 cm.
726 divided by 6 = 121   11 x 11 = 121 (They know ten times ten is 100, so it has to be a number greater than 10.)

Day 122 (die, quarter)
Probability

They wanted Jesus to prophesy who hit Him. (Matthew 26:59-68)

A.   Jesus didn't have to guess who was hitting Him. He knew or could have known. He wasn't going to obey their commands, though. If there was only one person there, would you be able to guess who was hitting you? **yes** It would certainly be that one person. If it were pouring rain outside and you didn't have an umbrella, what are the chances you would get wet if you went outside? **certain, 100%** It's completely certain that you would get wet.

We are talking about how probable things are. Things can be certain. Things can be impossible. Things can be likely or unlikely. Can you think of some examples of what would be impossible chances, like the chances of staying dry while standing in the pouring rain without an umbrella?

Example: choosing an apple to eat for lunch when you are out of apples
Actually, I hate talking about impossible odds, because I think there's always a chance. There are few things that are actually impossible. I know a missionary whose daughter really wanted an apple and they had no money to buy any. They opened their front door and there was a bag of apples. The impossible probability of her having an apple for lunch turned into a certainty. But we are talking about this mathematically. The chances of you waking up tomorrow on Mars is impossible.

By the way, speaking mathematically, it's impossible for the world to randomly form itself from a Big Bang. Scientists know this. It can be proven mathematically.

Let's move on to likely and unlikely. What are some examples of likely and unlikely events, such as it's likely to rain when it's really cloudy out and unlikely that it will be a warm sunny day.

Example: If your mom needs three helpers and there are four kids hanging around, it's likely you'll be asked to help, and unlikely you won't be.

B.   Roll a die over and over again and jot down a tally mark in each column when that number comes up. Do it about thirty times.

Did one number come up more than the others?

Is it more likely that one number would come up compared to another number? **No**

Just because one number came up more often doesn't mean it's more likely to come up. Each number has the same chance, a one out of six chance.

If you rolled the die right now one time, is it likely or unlikely that you'll roll a two?

unlikely

Would it be likely or unlikely that you didn't roll a two?

likely

Roll the die one more time and see what happens.

C.   Flip a coin twenty times. Record what side it lands on each time. What is the outcome? What should be the outcome?

There should be an even number. There is an even chance of either side coming up.

What's the chance of a head coming up?

There are two possibilities. The head is one of the two possibilities. The tail is one of the two possibilities. There is a one out of two chance of a head coming up.

You can write that as a fraction. $^1/_2$

If there was one red, one blue, and one yellow marble in a bowl, and you picked one out, what are the chances you picked out the blue one?

one out of three, $^1/_3$

D.   There are two red marbles, three blue marbles, one yellow marble, four green marbles, and five white marbles in a bowl. What is the probability of each color being chosen at random? Write the answers as fractions. Can you reduce any of those fractions to make equivalent fractions with smaller denominators? (Hint: You can look to see if the numerator divides into the denominator.)

$^2/_{15}$ chance of choosing a red marble $^3/_{15}$ chance of choosing a blue, 1/5

$^1/_{15}$ chance of choosing a yellow marble $^4/_{15}$ chance of choosing a green

$^5/_{15}$ chance of choosing a white marble reduces to 1/3

Day 123
Multiplication and Division

Peter denied Jesus three times. (Matthew 26:69-27-2)

A.   Let's do things three times again. If you were given $100 three times, how much would you have?

$300

What if you were given $120 dollars three times?

$360
That's just like being given $100 three times and $20 three times. You could demonstrate that with pretend $100 and $20 bills.

What if you were given $123 dollars three times?

$369
That's like getting $100 three times, $20 three times, and $3 three times. And they've already found out the first two of those.

B.   If you were given $1000 three times, how much would you have?

$3000

If you were given $1400 three times, how much would you have?

$4200

If you were given $1430 three times, how much would you have?

$4290

If you were given $1436 three times, how much would you have?

$4308

C.   If you were given $674 three times, how much would you have?

$2022

If you were given $49 thirty-three times, how much would you have?

$1617
49 x 33 OR 50 x 33 = 1500 + 150 = 1650 − 33 = 1617 Why?
It's easier to multiply by 50 than by 49. Multiplication is just adding over and over again. We added 33 fifty times. That was one too many, so we subtracted off one.

D.   If you were given $693 by someone giving you three gifts of the same amount, how much did they give you each time?

$231

If you were given $452 by someone giving you three gifts of almost the same amount except the last one had just a little more in it, how much did they give you each time and how much extra was in the last amount?

$150 and $2

If you were given $197 by someone giving you three gifts of almost the same amount except the last one had just a little more in it, how much did they give you each time and how much extra was in the last amount (hint: the remainder)?

$65 and $2

Day 124

Decimals

Judas was given thirty pieces of silver. (Matthew 26:3-14)

A.   If one piece of silver was worth $4.23, how much would two pieces be worth?

$4.23
+ $4.23
$8.46

If one piece of silver was worth $32.14, how much would two pieces be worth?

$32.14
+ $32.14
$64.28

If one piece of silver was worth $0.50, how much would two pieces be worth?

$1.00, 100 cents

If one piece of silver was worth $1.50, how much would two pieces be worth? (Hint: They can add the dollars and cents separately and then put them together. 100 cents equals one dollar.)

$3.00, 300 cents
1 dollar + 1 dollar + 50 cents + 50 cents

B.   If one piece of silver was worth $10.50, how much would two pieces be worth?

$21
10 + 10 + 50 cents + 50 cents

If one piece of silver was worth $6.47, how much would two pieces be worth?

$6.47
+ $6.47
$12.94
$6 + $6 + 40 cents + 40 cents + 7 cents + 7 cents = $12 + 94 cents

If one piece of silver was worth $23.61, how much would two pieces be worth?

$23.61
+ $23.61
$47.22
$20 + $20 + $3 + $3 + 60 cents + 60 cents + 1 cent + 1 cent = $46 + 122 cents

If one piece of silver was worth $40.75, how much would two pieces be worth?

$40.75
+ $40.75
$81.50
$40 + $40 + 70 cents + 70 cents + 5 cents + 5 cents = $80 + 150 cents

C. If one piece of silver was worth $46.99, how much would two pieces be worth?

$46.99
+ $46.99
$93.98
$40 + $40 + $6 + $6 + 90 cents + 90 cents + 9 cents + 9 cents = $92 + 198 cents

If one piece of silver was worth $128.27, how much would two pieces be worth?

$128.27
+ $128.27
$256.54
$100 + $100 + $20 + $20 + $8 + $8 + 20 ¢ + 20 ¢ + 7 ¢ + 7 ¢ = $256 + 54 ¢

If one piece of silver was worth $135.90, how much would two pieces be worth?

$135.90
+ $135.90
$271.90
$100 + $100 + $30 + $30 + $5 + $5 + 90 cents + 90 cents = $270 + 180 cents

If one piece of silver was worth $281.50, how much would two pieces be worth?

$281.50
+ $281.50
$563.00
$200 + $200 + $80 + $80 + $1 + $1 + 50 cents + 50 cents = $562 + 100 cents

D.   If one piece of silver was worth $890.67, how much would two pieces be worth?

$890.67
+ $890.67
$1781.34
$800 + $800 + $90 + $90 + 60 ¢+ 60 ¢ + 7 ¢ + 7 ¢ = $1780 + 134 ¢

If one piece of silver was worth $567.89, how much would two pieces be worth?

$567.89
+ $567.89
$1135.78
$500 + $500 + $60 + $60 + $7 + $7 + 80 ¢+ 80 ¢ + 9 ¢ + 9 ¢ = $1134 + 178 ¢

If one piece of silver was worth $2671.53, how much would two pieces be worth?

$2671.53
+ $2671.53
$5343.06
$2000 + $2000 + $600 + $600 + $71 + $71 + 50¢ + 50¢ + 3¢ + 3¢ = $5342 + 106¢

If one piece of silver was worth $9999.99, how much would two pieces be worth?

$9999.99
+ $9999.99
$19999.98
Think about it. They are each one cent short of ten thousand. Two ten thousands is twenty thousand. So the answer is two cents less than twenty thousand. There is no need to even write out the equation.

Day 125
Review

A.   In a perfect cube each of the six sides is a square. If each side had an area of 5 meters squared, what would be the total surface area of the cube?

30 meters squared

Is it likely or unlikely that you will be asked to help if there are twenty people there, and they only need one helper?

unlikely

How much would you have if you were given $231 dollars three times?

$693
That's like getting $200 three times, $30 three times, and $3 three times.

If one piece of silver was worth $21.43, how much would two pieces be worth?

   $21.43
+ $21.43
   $42.86

If one piece of silver was worth $0.50, how much would two pieces be worth?

$1.00, 100 cents

B. What would be the surface area of a cube where each side had a length of five centimeters?

150 cm²
5 x 5 = 25 (one side), six times

If you had six quarters, how much money would you have?

$1.50 (6 x 25, just like the previous question)

If you rolled two dice right now, is it likely or unlikely that you'd roll a four?

unlikely

Would it be likely or unlikely that you rolled a number over two?

likely

If you were given $2375 three times, how much would you have?

$7125

If one piece of silver was worth $45.70, how much would two pieces be worth?

$45.70
+ $45.70
$91.40
$40 + $40 + $5 + $5 + 70 cents + 70 cents = $90 + 140 cents

C. What would be the surface area of a cube where each side had a length of thirty-eight inches?

8664 in²
38 x 38 = 1444(one side), six times
30 x 38 and 8 x 38 = 900 + 240 and 240 + 64 = 1300 + 140 + 4

What's the chance of a tail coming up when you flip a coin? (Write it as a fraction.)

¹/₂

If there was one red, one blue, and one yellow marble in a bowl, and you picked one out, what are the chances you picked out the red one?

one out of three, ¹/₃

If you were given $498 three times, how much would you have?

$1494
400 x 3 and 90 x 3 and 8 x 3 = 1200 + 270 + 24 = 1400 + 90 + 4

If one piece of silver was worth $367.81, how much would two pieces be worth?

  $367.81
+ $367.81
  $735.62
$300 + $300 + $60 + $60 + $7 + $7 + 81 cents + 81 cents = $734 + 162 cents

D.   If the surface area of a cube were 3750 cm^2, what is the length of one side?

25 cm.
3750 divided by 6 = 625

Groups	Total
	3750
600	- 3600
	150
20	- 120
	30
5	30
625	0

25 x 25 = 625
(20 x 20 = 400 30 x 30 = 900 It has to be in between and 5 x 5 will give you 25.)

There are two yellow marbles, three red marbles, one blue marble, four white marbles, and five green marbles in a bowl. What is the probability of each color being chosen at random? Write the answers as fractions. Can you reduce any of those fractions to make equivalent fractions with smaller denominators? (Hint: If both numbers are even, you can at least divide the top and bottom, the numerator and denominator by two.)

^{2}/15 **chance of choosing a yellow marble**

^{3}/15 **chance of choosing a red marble, ^{1}/5**

^{1}/15 **chance of choosing a blue marble**

^{4}/15 **chance of choosing a white marble**

^{5}/15 **chance of choosing a green marble, ^{1}/3**

If you were given $347 by someone giving you three gifts of almost the same amount except the last one had just a little more in it, how much did they give you each time and how much extra was in the last amount (hint: the remainder)?

$115 and $2

If one piece of silver was worth $3948.25, how much would two pieces be worth?

$3948.75
+ $3948.75
 $7897.50
$3000 + $3000 + $900 + $900 + $40 + $40 + $8 + $8 + 70¢ + 70¢ + 5¢ + 5¢ = $7896 + 150¢

Day 126

Fractions

A riot was starting. (Matthew 27:24-31)

A.   What if half of a crowd of twenty people were starting to riot? How many people were causing trouble?

10 people because 10 is half of 20

What if half of a crowd of fifty people were starting to riot? How many people were causing trouble? (Hint: What two coins make fifty cents? **two quarters**)

25 people because 25 is half of 50

What if half of a crowd of eighteen people were starting to riot? How many people were causing trouble?

9 people because 9 is half of 18

What if half of a crowd of 100 people were starting to riot? How many people were causing trouble? (Hint: What's fifty cents plus fifty cents? **100 cents**)

50 people because 50 is half of 100

B.   Draw a crowd of ten people. Probably best to just draw ten lines. Circle three of them and write the fraction and decimal shown by the picture. Circle one more and write that fraction. Do the same thing two more times.

$3/10$ 0.3, $4/10$ 0.4, $5/10$ 0.5, $6/10$ 0.6

C.   Draw a box and divide into four parts. Color in one part. What fraction is shown?
one fourth Color in another box. What fraction is shown? **two fourths** You just
added one fourth and one fourth and got two fourths. What changed? What didn't
change?

**You added the numerators together 1 + 1 = 2 but the number of parts, the
denominator didn't change.**

Add together the four fractions you wrote in the previous section.

$^{18}/_{10}$

3 + 4 + 5 + 6 = 18 and the number of parts doesn't change. What number is equal
to 10 out of 10 parts?

1 whole

If you had ten squares and ten were colored in, you'd have one whole. Take out
ten of those pieces from the numerator of eighteen tenths and how many would
you have left?

8 pieces
18 − 10 = 8

What mixed number does eighteen tenths equal? Remember that a mixed
number is a whole number and a fraction together.

$1\,^{8}/_{10}$

Each of the fractions below is an equivalent fraction to either three tenths, four
tenths, five tenths, or six tenths. An equivalent fraction is an equal fraction, like
$^{1}/_{2} = ^{2}/_{4}$. You can draw a picture of a box and divide into four parts and then
color in half of it to show that it is true. Write the equivalent fraction of each of
these fractions.

$^{6}/_{20} = ^{3}/_{10}$ $^{3}/_{5} = ^{6}/_{10}$ $^{1}/_{2} = ^{5}/_{10}$ $^{9}/_{30} = ^{3}/_{10}$

Bonus: Reduce eight tenths. Make the numerator and denominator smaller. (Hint:
any time they are both even, you can always divide them each by two, just divide
in half.)

4/5

D. Each of these fractions is an equivalent fraction to either three tenths, four tenths, five tenths, or six tenths. Write the equivalent fraction of each of these fractions.

$2/5 = 4/10$ $36/60 = 6/10$ $20/40 = 5/10$ $6/15 = 4/10$

The last one was tricky. 6 and 15 both divide by three making them 2 and 5, and they already found that two fifths is equivalent to four tenths.

Now find another equivalent fraction for each of them. Reduce each fraction as far as you can.

$2/5$ $3/5$ $1/2$ $2/5$

Now add together all of these new equivalent fractions (two fifths, etc.) To start you are going to have to give them all a common denominator. It's always easiest to find the least common denominator. Here it will be ten. Write your answer as a mixed number.

$19/10$ $1\,9/10$

Add this mixed number with your previous answer of one and eight tenths. Reduce the fraction if possible.

$2\,17/10$ $3\,7/10$

The fraction can't be reduced.

Day 127
Fractions

They divided His clothes. (Matthew 27:32-40)

A.   They divided Jesus' clothes. They didn't rip up his clothes, but let's say they did. Let's say they took his cloak and divided it in half. How many pieces would they have divided it into?

2

Let's say they took his cloak and divided it in thirds. How many pieces would they have divided it into?

3

Let's say they took his cloak and divided it in fourths. How many pieces would they have divided it into?

4

Let's say they took his cloak and divided it in sevenths. How many pieces would they have divided it into?

7

If they divided it into nine pieces, how do you think you would say that?

ninths

Can you write one ninth as a fraction? (Hint: One tenth looks like this $^1/_{10}$.)

$^1/_9$

B.   If one soldier got two fifths of His cloak and then won three fifths of the cloak in a bet, how much of the cloak would he have? Write the fractions, add them, then answer the question. Draw a picture to help you.

$^2/_5 + {}^3/_5 = {}^5/_5 = 1$
You would have all five of the five pieces, one cloak.

If one soldier got two sevenths of His cloak and then won four sevenths of the cloak in a bet, how much of the cloak would he have? Write the fractions, add them, then answer the question. You can draw a picture to help you.

$2/7$ + $4/7$ = $6/7$ = 6 of the 7 pieces

If one soldier got one ninth of His cloak and then won four ninths of the cloak in a bet, how much of the cloak would he have? Write the fractions, add them, then answer the question. You can draw a picture to help you.

$1/9$ + $4/9$ = $5/9$ = 5 of the 9 pieces

If one soldier got three eighths of His cloak and then won four eighths of the cloak in a bet, how much of the cloak would he have? Write the fractions, add them, then answer the question. You can draw a picture to help you.

$3/8$ + $4/8$ = $7/8$ = 7 of the 8 pieces

C. If a soldier had three pieces of clothing and two thirds of another and then lost in a bet one piece and one third of another, how much did he have left? Write the equation and answer with mixed numbers.

$3\,^2/_3$ - $1\,^1/_3$ = $2\,^1/_3$

Three minus one equals two. Two thirds minus one third equals one third because two minus one equals one. If you drew a circle and divided it into three parts and put a dot in two of the parts, that would represent two thirds of the circles. If you took one of the dots away (minus one), then you would be left with one circle with a dot in it, one of the three, one third.

If a soldier had fourteen pieces of clothing and three fifths of another and then lost in a bet eight pieces and one fifth of another, how much did he have left? Write the equation and answer with mixed numbers.

$14\,^3/_5$ – $8\,^1/_5$ = $6\,^2/_5$

Fourteen minus eight equals six. Three minus one equals two. The denominator, the number of total pieces doesn't change.

If a soldier had thirty pieces of clothing and seven ninths of another and then lost in a bet sixteen pieces and two ninths of another, how much did he have left? Write the equation and answer with mixed numbers.

$$30 \, ^7/_9 \; - \; 16 \, ^2/_9 \; = \; 14 \, ^5/_9$$

If a soldier had twelve fifths of the clothing and then lost in a bet six fifths of another, how much did he have left? Write the equation and answer with improper fractions (where the numerator is bigger than the denominator) and then again with mixed numbers.

$$^{12}/_5 \; - \; ^6/_5 \; = \; ^6/_5 \; = \; 1 \, ^1/_5$$

D. If one soldier got three fifths and another got four times as many pieces, how many pieces did he get? Write the answer as an improper fraction and as a mixed number. When you multiply fractions by a whole number, the denominator will not change. You're only dealing with the number of pieces out of the whole. You'll multiply the numerator times four. The denominator will stay the same.

$$^{12}/_5 \quad 2 \, ^2/_5$$

If you take out one whole, five pieces, you still have seven fifths, an improper fraction. You have to take out another whole, another five pieces, so you have a total of two wholes, or two.

12 − 5 = 7 (take out one whole)   7 − 5 = 2 (take out another whole, two pieces left)

(Note: You could review here how when you multiply fractions you multiply the numerators together and the denominators together. When you have a whole number, it's like there's an invisible one in the denominator. That's why the denominator stays the same.)

If one soldier got seven twelfths and another got fourteen times as many pieces, how many pieces did he get? Write the answer as an improper fraction and as a mixed number. Reduce the fraction in the mixed number if it is possible.

$$^{98}/_{12} \quad 8 \, ^2/_{12} \quad 8 \, ^1/_6$$

Divide 12 into 98 to see how many wholes you can take out of it.

If both numbers are even, you can always divide them both by two to reduce the fraction and find an equivalent fraction. Remember that all of those answers are equal amounts.

If one soldier got nine fifths and another got seventeen times as many pieces, how many pieces did he get? Write the answer as an improper fraction and as a mixed number. Reduce the fraction in the mixed number if it is possible.

$153/5$ $30\,3/5$

30 times 5 = 150 and then there are three pieces left over.

How do you think you would multiply $3\,5/6$ by eight?

$30\,2/3$ $3 \times 8 = 24$ and $5 \times 8 = 40$ $24\,40/6 = 30\,4/6$

Can you divide 4 and 6 each by the same number to reduce the fraction and get an equivalent fraction?

$30\,2/3$

Day 128
Fractions

They were mocking Jesus. (Matthew 27:41-49)

A.   I don't have a math lesson for mocking. That doesn't sound nice, so I want to keep doing fractions. Today you are going to write fractions with a denominator of five. That means they will all have the number five on the bottom.

Here is the fraction one half, ½ .   I write it crooked because it's easiest to type it that way. Draw a picture that shows one half.

any shape divided in half with one half colored in

There are two parts and one is colored in. The number one half is talking about one of two parts.

What part of your hand has five parts to it?

your fingers

Hold up your left hand. Hold onto your left thumb with your right hand. How many of the five fingers are you holding onto? **one** What is the fraction that tells us how many of the five fingers you are holding onto?

$1/5$ one fifth, one of the five fingers They can just tell you the answer at first.

Now hold your thumb and one finger. How many of the five fingers are you holding? **two** What fraction tells us how many of the five fingers you are holding?

$2/5$ two fifths

Repeat with three, four, and five fingers.

We can write five fifths as just the number one. When you are holding all the fingers, you have one whole group of five fingers.

Write out those fifths you just answered, from one fifth to five fifths.

$1/5$ $2/5$ $3/5$ $4/5$ $5/5$ or 1

B.   Add together the fractions you just wrote.

15/5

If you had fifteen fingers, how many hands would you have?

3

Draw five circles. Color in one of them. Color in half of each of the other circles. Add together the colored parts. How much do you have? Write the equation and the answer. 1 + ½ + ... =

1 + ½ + ½ + ½ + ½ = 3

If you had four and a half circles colored in and then erased one and a half of them, how many would be colored in?

3

C.   Subtract forty and seven eighths minus twelve and three eighths.

28 $^4/_8$ = 28 ½ because 4 is half of 8

D.   Think! How would you subtract 7 $^1/_4$ - 4 $^5/_8$?

2 $^5/_8$

Let them try it before you go through this. If they didn't get it, have them write out the steps as you read through this.

You could think of it different ways. First you need to get common denominators, make them the same. How can you change the four into an eight? **4 x 2 = 8** You need to multiply the numerator and denominator by the same number to get an equivalent, equal, fraction. Why? **because any number over itself is the same as 1 and any number times 1 is just itself, the value doesn't change** One fourth times two over two is two eighths. Two eighths equals one fourth.

Now you could borrow one from the seven and add eight eighths to two eighths and get six and ten eighths. Then 6 − 4 = 2 and $^{10}/_8$ - $^5/_8$ = $^5/_8$

Or you could subtract two eighths minus five eighths and get negative three eighths. Then $7 - 4 = 3$ and you'd have to combine that with $-{}^3/_8$. If you take away 3 parts of 8 how many are left? 5 of the 8 parts, ${}^5/_8$.

Here's one more to try. $8\,{}^1/_3 - 3\,{}^4/_6$

$4\,{}^4/_6 = 4\,{}^2/_3$

You'll start with the equation $8\,{}^2/_6 - 3\,{}^4/_6$.

5 and $-{}^2/_6 = 4\,{}^4/_6$ because if you take away two parts from six you are left with four

OR $7\,{}^8/_6 - 3\,{}^4/_6 = 4\,{}^4/_6$

Four and six are both even so the fraction can certainly be reduced by dividing the top and bottom by two.

Day 129
Fractions

The veil was torn in two from top to bottom. (Matthew 27:50-56)

A.   What fraction describes one of the two pieces of the torn veil if it were torn in half?

½

Draw a picture that shows six out of seven things, six sevenths, $6/7$.

Draw a picture that shows three out of four parts of one whole object, three fourths, $3/4$.

The first should have seven objects, like seven lines with six of them circled. The second should have something like a square or a circle divided into four parts with three colored in. Answers will vary.

B.   Add one and one fourth plus three and two fourths.

$4\,^3/_4$

Add twenty-five and one fifth plus seventeen and three fifths.

$42\,^4/_5$

If the veil was torn in two, and one part was $^1/_8$ of the whole curtain, what fraction shows the size of the other piece? (Note: You might need to draw a picture to show them this. They are trying to make one whole out of two pieces.)

$^7/_8$

There would be seven parts left over. Say it measured 8 meters across. One eighth would be one meter. The other piece would then be 7 meters across.

If the veil was torn in two, and one part was $^3/_{14}$ of the whole curtain, what fraction shows the size of the other piece?

$^{11}/_{14}$

There would be 11 parts left in the other piece.

C. Find the difference between one hundred and seven fifteenths and thirty-four and two fifteenths.

66 $^5/_{15}$ = 66 $^1/_3$
100 – 34 = 66, 7 – 2 = 5, 1 x 5 = 5 and 3 x 5 = 15 You can take the five out of the numerator and denominator, and you are left with 1 and 3. You are officially dividing when you do that.

Find the difference between fifty-two and eight fifteenths and seven and three fifteenths.

45 $^5/_{15}$ = 45 $^1/_3$
52 – 7 = 45, 8 – 3 = 5, 1 x 5 = 5 and 3 x 5 = 15

Find the sum of seven twelfths and eight twelfths. Write your answer as an improper fraction and then as a mixed number. Then reduce the fractional part of the mixed number. (Hint: 3 x 1 = 3 and 3 x 4 = 12)

$^{15}/_{12}$ = 1 $^3/_{12}$ = 1 $^1/_4$
Take out 1 which is twelve twelfths. If you take away twelve parts, there are three parts left.

D. Multiply four fifths times six sevenths. When you multiply fractions, you multiply the numerators together and you multiply the denominators together.

$^4/_5$ x $^6/_7$ = $^{24}/_{35}$

Multiply four sixths times five eighths.

$^4/_6$ x $^5/_8$ = $^{20}/_{48}$ = $^{10}/_{24}$ = $^5/_{12}$
If you were vigilant, you could see that four sixths could become two thirds and change that even before you multiplied.

Multiply five halves by six ninths.

$^5/_2$ x $^6/_9$ = $^{30}/_{18}$ = $^{10}/_6$ = $^5/_3$ = 1 $^2/_3$
Multiply the numerators, denominators. Divide top and bottom to reduce. Take out 1.

Day 130
Review

A.   What if half of a crowd of forty people were starting to riot? How many people were causing trouble? (Hint: What would be half of four groups of people? Each group would have ten people in it.)

20

Let's say they took Jesus' cloak and divided it in ninths. How many pieces would they have divided it into?

9

How would you write one eighth as a fraction?

$1/8$

How would you write three fifths as a fraction?

$3/5$

Draw a picture that shows five out of six things, five sixths, $5/6$.

It should have six objects, like six lines with five of them circled.

Draw a picture that shows one out of four parts of one whole object, one fourth, $1/4$.

It should have something like a square or a circle divided into four parts with one colored in. Answers will vary.

B.   Draw a crowd of ten people. Probably best to just draw ten lines. Circle seven of them and write the fraction and decimal shown by the picture.

$7/10$ 0.7

If one soldier got two ninths of His cloak and then won five ninths of the cloak in a bet, how much of the cloak would he have? Write the fractions, add them, then answer the question. You can draw a picture to help you.

$2/9 + 5/9 = 7/9 =$ **7 of the 9 pieces**

If you had six and a half circles colored in and then erased two and a half of them, how many would be colored in?

4

Add twenty and one fifth plus seven and two fifths.

27 $3/5$

If the veil was torn in two, and one part was $1/12$ of the whole curtain, what fraction shows the size of the other piece?

$11/12$
There would be eleven parts left over. 12 – 1 = 11

C.   What mixed number does seventeen tenths equal? Remember that a mixed number is a whole number and a fraction together.

$1\,^7/_{10}$

Can you fill in the blank in the equivalent fraction?

$^8/_{40} = \,^?/_{10}$ $^1/_2 = \,^?/_{24}$ $^1/_5 = \,^?/_{25}$

2   **12**   **5**

$10 \times 4 = 40$ and $2 \times 4 = 8$ $2 \times 12 = 24$ and $1 \times 12 = 12$ $5 \times 5 = 25$ and $1 \times 5 = 5$

If a soldier had fourteen fifths of the clothing and then lost in a bet two fifths of another, how much did he have left? Write the equation and answer with improper fractions (where the numerator is bigger than the denominator) and then write the answer as a mixed number.

$^{14}/_5 - \,^2/_5 = \,^{12}/_5 = 2\,^2/_5$

Subtract thirty and four eighths minus twenty-four and one eighth.

$6\,^3/_8$

Find the sum of seven fifteenths and eleven fifteenths. Write your answer as an improper fraction and then as a mixed number. Then reduce the fractional part of the mixed number. (Hint: $3 \times 1 = 3$ and $3 \times 5 = 15$)

$^{18}/_{15} = 1\,^3/_{15} = 1\,^1/_5$

Take out 1 which is fifteen fifteenths. If you take away fifteen parts, there are three parts left over.

D.   Fill in the blank in the equivalent fractions.

$2/5 = ?/10$ $36/60 = ?/10$ $20/40 = 5/?$
4   **6**   **10**
5 x 2 = 10 and 2 x 2 = 4   10 x 6 = 60 and 6 x 6 = 36   10 x 4 = 40 and 5x4=20

If one soldier got seven fifteenths and another got nineteen times as many pieces, how many pieces did he get? Write the answer as an improper fraction and as a mixed number. Reduce the fraction in the mixed number if it is possible.

$133/15$ $8\,13/15$

Start with seven times nineteen. Then divide 15 into 133 to see how many wholes you can take out of it. It can't be reduced.

Multiply $5\,4/9$ by three.

16 1/3   5 x 3 = 15 and 4 x 3 = 12 $15\,12/9 = 15 + 1\,1/3 = 16\,1/3$
                                         $12/9 = 1\,3/9 = 1\,1/3$

   12 − 9 = 3 (take out one whole and three pieces out of nine are still left over.) Multiply the whole number. Multiply the fraction. Put them together. Reduce by dividing top and bottom by 3. Remember when you divide by 1 it's just the same number, nothing changes. Any number over itself is just 1. That's why we can multiply or divide by any number over itself and get an equivalent, equal, fraction.

$7\,1/3 - 3\,4/9 = \mathbf{3\,8/9}$

Multiply seven halves by eight ninths.

$7/2$ x $8/9$ = $56/18$= $3\,2/18$= $3\,1/9$
Multiply the numerators, denominators. Take out 1s. Reduce

Days 131 - 140
Each workbook level has its own problems.

A.

Day 131
Arithmetic: 90, 800, 17
Fractions: 1/3 >2/3
Time: 6 hours

Day 132
Arithmetic: 80, 100, 12
Geometry: square, triangle
Fractions: 1/6 <5/6

Day 133
Arithmetic: 32, 478, 8
Measurement: 1000 millimeters
Word problem: 82 talents
Word problem: lost ten

Day 134
Arithmetic: 13, 186, 5
Percent: $2, $3
Roman numerals: 10, 12, 15, 17

Day 135
Line one: $23.30, $46.60
Line two: $14.12, $28.24
Line three: $693
Line four: $396
Line five: $42.86
Line six: $84.02

A.

Day 136
Arithmetic: 211, 78, 16
Measurement: 50 miles
Word problem: 40 bags of cookies

Day 137
Arithmetic: 34, 15, 7
Time: 4:30
Elapsed time: 30 minutes

Day 138
Arithmetic: 24, 88, 9
Word problem: 60 meters squared
Probability: likely
Money: $1

Day 139
Arithmetic: 333, 169, 15
Word problem: 10 people
Word problem: 5 pieces
Fractions: 3/7
Fractions: A picture like eight circles with five circles colored in.
Fractions: Draw a picture like a box with two lines, making three parts, then color in one part.

Day 140
Line one: $43.20, $86.40
Line two: $12.10, $24.20
Line three: $600
Line four: $309
Line five: $28.60
Line six: $86.20

B.

Day 131
Subtraction: $2.75, 275
Addition: $11.35, 1135
Fractions: Answers will vary but the answer to the addition problem should have the same
       numerator and denominator.
Time: 9:45

Day 132
Subtraction: $2.36, 236
Addition: $4.94, 494
Time: eight and a half hours, three and a half hours
Geometry: sphere

Day 133
Subtraction: $2.95, 295
Addition: $8.15, 815
Measurement: 4 cups
Word problem: 138 talents
Negative numbers: lost 4, -4

Day 134
Subtraction: $4.07, 607
Addition: $20.63, 1063
Percent: $5, $0.50
Difference: $4.50
Roman numerals: 9, 14

Day 135
Line one: $44.01
Line two: $43.84
Line three: $9474
Line four: $73.60

B.

Day 136
Subtraction: $6.15, 615
Addition: $9.25, 925
Word problem: 6 bags
Time: two hours and fifteen minutes

Day 137
Subtraction: $5.61, 561
Addition: $12.09, 1209
Measurement: 800 miles
Surface area: area of one side 10 x 10 = 100, six sides = 600
Probability: unlikely

Day 138
Subtraction: $4.48, 448
Addition: $14.72, 1472
Fraction: 3/10
Fractions: 2/9 + 3/9 = 5/9 of the cloak

Day 139
Subtraction: $1.74, 174
Addition: $11.40, 1140
Mixed numbers: 5 circles
Mixed numbers: 29 5/8
Fractions: 8/9

Day 140
Line one: $32.90
Line two: $40.17
Line three: $7311
Line four: $101

C.

Day 131
Fractions: 3/5
Time: 7 hours 38 minutes, 6 hours 3 minutes
Geometry: NOT polygons: The figures with a curved side, the figure that is open on one side, the circle

Day 132
Measurement: 32 cups
Roman numerals: XXXIX, CCLXII
Arithmetic: 971, $0.24, 2496

Day 133
Word problem: $159.80
Word problem: $457
Arithmetic: 840, 279, $0.38, 4424

Day 134
Area: one side is 67 x 67 = 4489, all six sides = 26,934 in^2
Probability: ½
Probability: 1/3
Arithmetic: 1161, 139, $0.61; 96,000

Day 135
Word problem: $1728
Word problem: $499.12
Word problem: 1673 bags of cookies
Arithmetic: 1292, 366, $0.54

C.

Day 136
Word problem: 2583 talents
Word problem: -69, lost 69 talents
Percent: $8.80, $8.08, $770, $707
      (1 percent: move decimal over two places, 10 percent is one decimal place over.)
Arithmetic: 1117, 198, $0.59

Day 137
Measurement: 2160 miles
Time: 13 hours 38 minutes
Arithmetic: 1086, 183, 88, 2618

Day 138
Fractions: 19/10, 1 9/10
Fractions: 2, 6
Fractions: 13/5 − 2/5 = 11/5 = 2 1/5
Arithmetic: 1100, 189, $0.26, 2754

Day 139
Fractions: 11 3/8
Fractions: 25/15, 1 10/15, 1 2/3
Arithmetic: 8700, 290, 155,000

Day 140
Word problem: $1185
Word problem: $567.48
Word problem: 1992 bags of cookies
Arithmetic: 1427, 54, $0.73

D.

Day 131
Fractions: 3/12 x 3 = 9/12 = ¾
Time: 6 hours 53 minutes, 12 hours 25 minutes
Multiply: 143,250

Day 132
Measurement: 1/8
Multiply: 1008
Geometry: The ones on the left have two parallel lines. The trapezoid has one. The curved
shape has none.

Day 133
Multiply: 332
Fractions: 4 2/9
Fractions: 72/27 = 2 18/27 = 2 2/3
Measurement: 1050 miles
Word problem: 332

Day 134
Word problem: 7/15 x 19 = 133/15 = 8 13/15
Multiply fractions: 5 x 3 = 15, 4/9 x 3 = 12/9 = 1 3/9 = 1 1/3, 15 and 1 1/3 = 16 1/3
Percent: $4.80
Roman Numerals: MCMXXXI, MMDCCLIX
Multiply: 131,130

Day 135
Divide: 31,926 ; 3.1926 ; .31926 ; .031926 ; .0031926
Divide: 34
Multiply: 6170

D.

Day 136
Money: $7896.50
Fractions: 4, 6, 10
Negative number: - 1174, 1174 lost
Percent: $26.46
Multiply: 51,102

Day 137
Probability: yellow 2/15, red 3/15 = 1/5, blue 1/15, white 4/15, green 5/15 = 1/3
Word problem: $115, $115, $117
Percentage: 50%
Word problem: 53 talents
Multiply: 178,560

Day 138
Time: 7 hours 41 minutes
Measurement: 625 is the area of one side, 25 x 25 = 625, answer: 25 centimeters
Multiply: 492,480

Day 139
Divide: 36
Word problem: 1008 bags of cookies
Word problem: 112 people
Arithmetic: $4.73, $7.19, $0.36

Day 140
Multiply: 425.83 ; 4258.3 ; 42,584 ; 425,830 ; 4,258,300
Divide: 59
Multiply: 44,786

These are the final 40 review/practice/mastery days. These are set up like the review weeks.

Days 141 - 150
Each workbook level has its own problems.

A.

Day 141
Arithmetic: 432, 63, 478, 78
Ordinals: Jacob
Skip count: 30
Time: 3:00
Time: AM

Day 142
Arithmetic: 113, 50, 499, 140
Ordinals: Isaac
Sip count: 28
Time: 1:00
Time: PM

Day 143
Arithmetic: 432, 90, 478, 120
Word problem: 11 miles
Word problem: 14 bushels
Geometry: a circle with a line down the middle or half colored in

Day 144
Arithmetic: 572, 60, 687, 100
Word problem: 7 miles
Word problem: 7 days
Double: 14, 20, 40

Day 145
Line one: 432, 40, 478, 120
Line two: 201, 90, 747, 160
Line three: 26, 80, 988, 130

A.

Day 146
Arithmetic: 701, 80, 868, 100
Word problem: 10 cookies
Negative numbers: $8

Day 147
Arithmetic: 331, 90, 597, 130
Place value: 4|5
Place value: 70
Expanded form: 50 + 7

Day 148
Arithmetic: 322, 80, 977, 110
Place value: 1|7
Place value: 40
Expanded form: 60 + 7

Day 149
Arithmetic: 500, 70 769, 140
Geometry: across the middle of the circle in any direction, across the middle of the rectangle top to bottom or side to side (not along the diagonal), from a point on the triangle to the middle of the opposite side
Word problem: 80 grapes

Day 150
Line one:1, 70, 378, 160
Line two: 141, 90, 898, 100
Line three: 510, 60, 879, 170

B.

Day 141
Arithmetic: 30, 40, 50, 58, 40, 53
Ordinals: Jacob
Skip counting: 16, 22
Time: 3:00
Time: PM

Day 142
Arithmetic: 55, 45, 815, 42, 74, 774
Ordinals: Judah
Skip counting: 15, 40
Time: 6:30
Time: AM

Day 143
Arithmetic: 61, 64, 996, 81, 74, 350
Word problem: 17 miles
Skip counting: 100
Time: 1:00

Day 144
Arithmetic: 67, 55, 914, 73, 75, 763
Word problem: 29 miles
Skip counting: 200
Time: 2:30

Day 145
Line one: 39, 60, 107, 67, 51, 1074
Line two: 60, 560, 71, 53, 75, 776
Line three: 42, 46, 584, 69, 63, 361
Line four: 63, 55, 910, 54, 60, 792
Bottom: 100

B.

Day 146
Arithmetic: 68, 7, 1, 8, 9, 98
Word problem: 20 bushels
Double: 160
Word problem: 56 miles

Day 147
Arithmetic: 9, 47, 70, 90, 80, 27
Word problem: 5 days
Fractions: should have four pretty similarly sized parts
Multiply: 64, 50, 200

Day 148
Arithmetic: 16, 45, 8, 90, 500, 9
Word problem: 30 things
Negative numbers: $11
Place value: 3|7|0, |4|6
Expanded form: 500 + 10 + 7

Day 149
Arithmetic: 65, 28, 543, 432, 32, 24
Symmetry: a circle, square, or rectangle would work, divided in half two ways
Difference: 43 yards
Word problem: 90 grapes

Day 150
Line one: 18, 743, 235, 1400
Line two: 38, 353, 439, 3600
Line three: 17, 667, 689, 1900
Bottom: 90, 70, 3000

C.

Day 141
Arithmetic: 4052, 7597, 7180, 1100
Multiply: 2856
Add: 225
Multiply line one: 24, 15, 18, 24
Multiply line two: 42, 49, 81, 64
Multiply line three: 30, 21, 32, 72

Day 142
Arithmetic: 4512, 8111, 185, 5857
Word problem: 253 bushels
Multiply:180
Multiply: 544
Multiply: 609

Day 143
Arithmetic: 1994, 6443, 9026, 826
Word problem: 44 ounces
Word problem: 3 days
Double: 150, 98, 300

Day 144
Arithmetic: 5933, 4986, 9292, 733
Word problem: 72 cards
Place value: 1|6|2|7
Expanded form: 4000 + 100 + 7
Standard form: 7508

Day 145
Line one: 621, 822, 745, 424
Line two: 5056, 7000, 554, 532
Line three: 630, 378, 246, 304
Bottom: 420

C.

Day 146
Arithmetic: 178, 476, 319, 72
Add: 603
Multiply: 51, 414
Multiply: 57, 390

Day 147
Arithmetic: 227, 365, 487, 418
Time: 1:55
Area: 48 blocks

Day 148
Arithmetic: 399, 37, 686, 350
Fractions: ¾
Negative numbers: $412
Multiply: 68, 768

Day 149
Arithmetic: 256, 789, 3849, 382
Geometry: 3
Difference: 446
Multiply: 108, 64

Day 150
Line one: 309, 758, 779, 78
Line two: 1860, 7666, 336, 72
Bottom: 60, 90
Multiply: 1484, 2569

D.

Day 141
Arithmetic: 5723, 9984, 602; 100,000
Time: 1:55
Hours: 720 hours
Word problem: 151 miles

Day 142
Arithmetic: 1237, 8418, 632; 100,000
Time: 10:11
Add: 898
Word problem: $1030

Day 143
Arithmetic: 7021, 1037, 1324, 4921
Numbers: 56,259
Expanded: 30,000 + 2000 + 100 + 70 + 9
Word problem: 5248 bushels

Day 144
Arithmetic: 15,723, 1421, 6323, 7149
Add: 1007
Multiply:4248
Area: 238 in.^{2}

Day 145
Line one: 8, 9, 6, 8
Line two: 7, 6, 6, 7
Line three: 368, 222, 196, 340
Line four: 810, 2132, 1833; 159,600
Divide: 78

D.

Day 146
Arithmetic: 2385, 3050, 1141, 4859
Word problem: 172 grams
Word problem: 80 days
Fractions: ¾

Day 147
Arithmetic: 1897, 2685, 1660, 800
Double: 952
Word problem: 1068 things
Add: 6642

Day 148
Arithmetic: 201, 264, 78, 2255
Symmetry: 2
Difference: 4254 meters
Word problem: 784 grapes

Day 149
Arithmetic: 213, 3510, 169, 280
Multiply: 23,680
Add: 1205
Area: 432 cm^2

Day 150
Line one: 9, 4, 7, 9
Line two: 4,6, 7, 5
Line three: 270, 296, 168, 356
Line four: 1036, 3116, 3190, 2813
Divide: 57 R 2

Days 151 – 160

A.

Day 151
Addition: 18, 10, 13. 15, 9, 10
Arithmetic: 113, 50, 499, 140
Perimeter: 37 meters
Degrees: Turn all the around.
Calendar: 12 months

Day 152
Addition: 12, 9, 12, 17, 13, 12
Arithmetic: 352, 50, 879, 110
Area: 15 blocks
Calendar: 7 days

Day 153
Subtraction: 8, 6, 7, 9, 5, 2
Arithmetic: 336, 90, 878, 130
Word problem: 7 workers
Word problem: 62 workers
Money: $1.00

Day 154
Subtraction: 6, 7, 5, 3, 7, 8
Arithmetic: 510, 60, 682, 110
Word problem: ½
Word problem: 140 steps

Day 155
Play store

A.

Day 156
Addition: 9, 11, 15, 11, 13, 12
Arithmetic: 100, 102, 100
Round: 30, 70, 80, 30
Estimate: 30 + 40 = 70 miles
Greater than/less than: 1>1/ , 1/2 > ¼

Day 157
Addition: 12, 10, 13, 12, 16, 12
Arithmetic: 104, 130, 140
Estimate: 80 − 30 = 50 miracles
Greater than/less than: 38<31, 600>300

Day 158
Subtraction: 9, 5, 6, 9, 9, 8
Arithmetic: 500, 50, 800, 140
Time: 5 hours
Negative numbers: 2

Day 159
Subtraction: 7, 5, 5, 8, 9, 9
Arithmetic: 22, 60, 999, 170
Double: 6, 60, 600
Blanks: 7, 8, 40, 8
Money: 30 cents

Day 160
Play store

B.

Day 151
Arithmetic: 711, 354, 790, 394
Perimeter: 52 miles
Area: 50 blocks
Degrees: turn all the way around, turn halfway around, turn a quarter of the way around

Day 152
Arithmetic: 972, 345, 702, 309
Calendar: 52 weeks
Word problem: 122 days

Day 153
Arithmetic: 673, 775, 870, 394
Word problem: 83 workers
Word problem: 90 workers

Day 154
Arithmetic: 639, 803, 210, 94
Money: $0.18
Fractions: ¼
Fractions: ¾

Day 155
Arithmetic: 495, 891, 408, 450
Play store

B.

Day 156
Arithmetic: 396, 479, 751, 4
Word problem: 75 flights
Rounding: 20, 40, 50, 30
Estimation: 80 + 60 = 140 km
Greater than/Less than: 2/3 < 1

Day 157
Arithmetic: 73, 35, 1005, 68 (subtract 600 and add one back on)
Estimation: 100 − 30 = 70 miracles
Greater than/Less than: 2897 < 3015, 130 < 132

Day 158
Arithmetic: 753, 45, 140, 301
Time: 10:30
Negative numbers: 31

Day 159
Arithmetic: 353, 35, 1200, 170
Word problem: 80 pieces
Subtraction: 800
Blanks: 25, 27

Day 160
Answers will vary.

C.

Day 151
Perimeter: 2195 cm
Area: 4292 in²
Protractor: Three lines

Day 152
Multiply: 3420, 3572 (3800 is 38 one hundred times. You only need 94, so you can subtract off 38 six times. 3800 minus the answer to 38 x 6)
Minutes: 2340
Word problem: 26 workers

Day 153
Arithmetic: 1267, 900, 1240, 72
Money: $4.17
Fractions: 6/15 < 9/15

Day 154
Arithmetic: 906, 83, 4512, 380
Word problem: 2133 steps
Rounding: 200, 400, 700, 700
Fractions: Answers will vary. Examples: 3/16 + 6/16 = 9/16, 12/16 − 3/16 = 9/16

Day 155
Line one: 1662, 4200; 20,370 ; 463
Line two: 1243, 700, 846, 42
Line three: 1585, 870, 4094

C.

Day 156
Arithmetic: 1061, $0.60, 5550, $0.52
Estimation: 90 − 40 = 50 miles
Estimation: 1400 miracles, 1260 miracles, 1288 miracles

Day 157
Arithmetic: 673, $0.70, 1051, $0.64
Greater than/less than: 27,011 > 26,978 ; 2776 > 2490
Time: 5 hours 12 minutes

Day 158
Arithmetic: 1000, $7.00, 2166, $0.29
Negative numbers: 206 (They don't have to add and subtract straight through. They can "add" the numbers in any order. It would be easy to combine − 75 and 72 to get -3.)
Word problem: 32,000
Blanks: 213, 456

Day 159
Word problem: $6.23
Arithmetic: 1075, $0.40, 4042, $0.62
Geometry: Answers will vary.

Day 160
Line one: 788, 700, 1026, $0.71
Line two: 375, 900, 1084, $0.83
Line three: 2140, 4256, 15,440

D.

Day 151

Geometry: Answers will vary. The coordinates are written (x, y), meaning the number across and then the number up and down. Down and to the left are negative numbers. The area is the number of blocks included in the shape. Add up half blocks along with whole blocks.

Perimeter: 154 x 6 = 924

Day 152

Arithmetic: 5403, $8.03 ; 10,021 ; $5.13

Money: $1.19

Multiply: 27

Fractions: 5/5 – 1/5 = 4/5

Day 153

Arithmetic: 2371, $4.70, 8263, $5.13

Multiply fractions: 60

Multiply: 14,945 ; 25,241

Day 154

Arithmetic: 3107, $7.30 ; 10,273 ; $6.84

Word problem: 458 workers

Blanks: 23, 1100

Day 155

Arithmetic: 4585, $8.40; 30,810 ; $7.16

Multiply: 108

Divide: 84 R 4

D.

Day 156
Word problems: 513 steps
Round: 400, 200, 900, 1000
Multiply: 1950
Divide: 33 R 10

Day 157
Multiply: 7 million
Divide: 7 hundred thousand
Estimation: 100 + 400 + 400 = 900 = 15 hours, 100 + 350 + 390 = 840 = 14 hours,
        100 + 353 + 387 = 840 = 14 hours
Multiply: 234
Divide: 47 R 19

Day 158
Arithmetic: -5
Estimation: 800 miracles, 680 miracles, 672 miracles
Multiply: 325
Divide: 35

Day 159
Arithmetic: 1824 (wheat) < 1972 (barley)
Time: 9 hours 27 minutes

Day 160
Arithmetic: 9040, $5.84; 14,868 ; $428
Multiply: 324
Divide: 46

Days 161 - 170

A.

Day 161
Arithmetic: 15, 150, 7, 70
Roman numerals: 5, 15, 2, 13
Decimals and fractions: 0.7, 7/10

Day 162
Arithmetic: 11, 110, 8, 80
Decimals: 0.1, 0.3, 0.5

Day 163
Arithmetic: 15, 150, 8, 80
Numbers: 436, 615
Multiplication: 70, 30, 140

Day 164
Arithmetic: 10, 100, 7, 70
Money: $0.01 + $0.10 = $0.11
Money: $0.45 + $0.33 = $0.78
Multiply: 4 x 6 = 24, 3 x 6 = 18

Day 165
Check: 33 + 14 = 47 wrong, 67 − 23 = 44 wrong
Arithmetic: 7,998 ; 1,555
Word problem: 24 legs

A.

Day 166
Arithmetic: 26, 79, 12
Negative numbers: $4
Fractions: ¼

Day 167
Arithmetic: 33, 89, 6
Money: $8
Money: $4.30
Word problem: 7 kilos

Day 168
Arithmetic: 13, 186, 12
Measurement: odd
Measurement: tons
Measurement: ounces

Day 169
Arithmetic: 80, 500, 9
Word problem: 120 guests
Word problem: 80 guests
Percent: 7%, 24%
Fraction: 1/5

Day 170
Check: 34 + 45 = 79, 89 − 36 = 53
Arithmetic: 7,786 ; 1,164
Word problem: 10 legs

B.

Day 161
Arithmetic: 106, 1060
Arithmetic: 180, 1800
Roman numerals: 12, 4
Roman numerals: 19, 9
Measurement: 7 ½ cm

Day 162
Arithmetic: 36, 360
Arithmetic: 9, 90
Fractions and decimals: 4/10, 9/10, 0.4, 0.9
Decimals: 0.1, 0.2, 0.3, 0.4, 0.5
Fractions: 5/10, 6/10, 7/10, 8/10

Day 163
Arithmetic: 85, 850
Arithmetic: 207, 2070
Numbers: 3264, 7020
Multiply: 150, 100

Day 164
Arithmetic:13, 130
Arithmetic: 49, 490
Negative numbers: 6, 8
Word problem: $219
Mixed numbers: 4 3/10, 20 2/3, 150 ½

Day 165
Check: 57 + 23 = 80 wrong, 564 − 48 = 516 wrong
Check: 216 + 156 = 372 wrong, 101 − 76 = 25 wrong
Arithmetic: 8467, 4348
Word problem: 8 + 24 = 32 legs

B.

Day 166
Arithmetic: $0.04, $1.06
Money: $2.35 + $4.27 = $6.62
Multiply: 6
Multiply: 20, 0, 200

Day 167
Arithmetic: $2.09, $6.94
Word problem: $6.74
Word problem: 123 tons
Word problem: 117 grams

Day 168
Arithmetic: $4.07, $7.55
Measurement: odd
Measurement: 100 kilograms

Day 169
Arithmetic: $7.06, $5.07
Word problem: 350 guests, 413 guests
Percent: 10%, 1%
Fractions: 5/8

Day 170
Check: 37 + 47 = 84 wrong, 472 − 63 = 409 wrong
Check: 545 + 150 = 695 wrong, 85 − 26 = 59 wrong
Arithmetic: 7090, 4982
Word problem: 300 legs

C.

Day 161
Arithmetic: 874, $0.53, 2146
Roman numerals: LXXIX, CCXLI
Measurement: Answers will vary.
Fractions and decimals: 12.7, 12 7/10

Day 162
Arithmetic: 840, $0.38, 4424
Decimals and fractions: 4 3/10, 4.3 and 21.5, 21 5/10
Greater than/less than: 7.6 > 6.9 and 10.9 > 9.6

Day 163
Numbers: 17,004 ; 235,071
Multiply: 2914, 2660

Day 164
Word problem: $387
Fractions: 18 1/3
Subtract: 459
Multiply: 3038

Day 165
Arithmetic: $0.70, $0.63
Subtract: $0.49, $0.82, $0.13
Word problem: $243.69

C.

Day 166
Multiply: 35,910
Multiply: 31,980
Check: 317, wrong

Day 167
Money: $25.26
Word problem: 1132 tons
Word problem: 1904 ounces

Day 168
Word problem: 11,020
Multiply: 23,680
Measurement: 4.2 kilograms, 1700 grams, 8.2 cm long

Day 169
Word problem: 87 guests
Word problem: 22 guests
Word problem 2304 guests

Day 170
Fractions and percent: $0.28 28/100, 28% and $4.00, 400/100, 400%
Decimals: $5.12 + $20.37 = $25.49, $20.37 - $5.12 = $15.25
Multiply: 584 x 9 = 5256

D.

Day 161
Arithmetic: MCMLIII, CDLXXIV
Measurement: Answers will vary. Fractions will be out of 16.
Multiply: 17,138

Day 162
Decimals: 0.01, 0.05, 0.10, 0.25
Decimals: 0.35, 68.02
Fractions: 35/100, 68 2/100 = 68 1/50 (not necessary)
Multiply: 25,088

Day 163
Numbers: 429,403 ; 12,674,013
Multiply: 29,944
Word problem: $544

Day 164
Arithmetic: 2275, $3.88
Mixed numbers: 4 4/9
Divide: 73 R 2

Day 165
Arithmetic: $2.26, $8.87, $5.39
Multiply: $123.80
Divide: 175 R 10 (That's 10 out of 20 or 10/20 which equals ½ which equals .5, so 175.5)
    That's not necessary. If you have a kid who likes this stuff, show them.

D.

Day 166
Multiply: 17,208
Divide: 26, 26 x 18 = 468

Day 167
Money: $226.04
Word problem: 347 grams
Measurement: A line that's 3.8 cm.
Multiply: 91/18 = 5 1/18

Day 168
Word problem: 28 pounds
Measurement: 13 pounds, 560 ounces
Fractions: 5 1/9

Day 169
Word problem: 984 guests
Word problem: 743 guests
Word problem: 598 − 46 = 552 guests
Multiply: 128 64/9 = 128 + 7 1/9 = 135 1/9

Day 170
Percent: $0.73
Percent: 800%
Fractions: 16/72 = 2/9 , 8/45
Multiply: 105, 72

Days 171 – 180

A.

Day 171
Arithmetic: 90, 800, 13
Fractions: 1/3 < 2/3
Time: 6 hours

Day 172
Arithmetic: 80, 100, 12
Geometry: a square has four equal sides, a rectangle has two sets of equal sides
Fractions: 1/7 < 6/7

Day 173
Arithmetic: 32, 478, 11
Measurement: 1000 millimeters
Word problem: 46 talents
Word problem: lost five talents

Day 174
Arithmetic: 13, 186, 11
Percent: $4, $8
Roman numerals: 5, 13, 16, 7

Day 175
Line one: $23.30, $46.60
Line two: $14.12, $28.24
Line three: $693
Line four: $396
Line five: $42.86
Line six: $84.02

A.

Day 176
Arithmetic: 211, 78, 12
Measurement: 100 miles
Word problem: 30 bags of cookies

Day 177
Arithmetic: 34, 375, 15
Time: 7:30
Time: 30 minutes

Day 178
Arithmetic: 24, 88, 11
Word problem: 60 meters squared
Probability: likely
Money: $1.00

Day 179
Arithmetic: 333, 169, 17
Word problem: 10 people
Word problem: 6 pieces
Fractions: 3/7
Fractions: something like eight lines and five circled
Fractions: something like a box divided into four parts with one colored in

Day 180
Line one: $43.20, $86.40
Line two: $12.10, $24.20
Line three: $600
Line four: $309
Line five: $28.60
Line six: $86.10

B.

Day 171
Arithmetic: $2.75, 275
Arithmetic: $11.35, 1135
Fractions: Answers will vary. To add up to one the answer should have the same numerator and denominator.
Time: 10:15

Day 172
Arithmetic: $2.36, 236
Arithmetic: $4.94, 494
Time: 6 hours 30 minutes, 6 hours 30 minutes
Geometry: pyramid

Day 173
Arithmetic: $2.95, 295
Arithmetic: $7.55, 755
Measurement: 4 cups
Word problem: 4 cups
Word problem: 138 talents
Word problem: - 8 talents, lost 8

Day 174
Arithmetic: $4.07, 607
Arithmetic: $20.63, 1063
Percent: $7, $0.7
Difference: $6.30
Roman numerals: 19, 24

Day 175
Line one: $44.01
Line two: $43.84
Line three: 9747
Line four: $35.80

B.

Day 176
Arithmetic: $6.15, 615
Arithmetic: $9.25, 925
Word problem: 5 bags
Time: 4 hours and 15 minutes

Day 177
Arithmetic: $5.61, 561
Arithmetic: $12.09, 1209
Measurement: 1000 miles
Surface area: 600 centimeters squared
Probability: likely

Day 178
Arithmetic: $4.48, 448
Arithmetic: $14.72, 1472
Fractions and decimals: 3/10, 0.3
Fractions: 2/9 + 3/9 = 5/9

Day 179
Arithmetic: $1.74, $174
Arithmetic: $11.40, 1140
Mixed numbers: 5 circles
Mixed numbers: 29 5/8
Fractions: 8/9

Day 180
Line one: $32.90
Line two: $40.17
Line three: $7311
Line four: $101

C.

Day 171
Fractions: 2/7
Time: 6 hours 58 minutes and 5 hours 45 minutes
Geometry: rectangle, square, triangle, octagon, pentagon, hexagon, and the closed shape
        with straight sides

Day 172
Measurement: 8 cups
Roman numerals: LXXXIX, CCXLIV
Arithmetic: 858, $0.76, 2726

Day 173
Word problem: $1598
Word problem: $45.70
Arithmetic: 754, 467, $0.38, 3276

Day 174
Area: 8214in^2
Probability: ½
Probability: likely
Arithmetic: 1121, 139, $0.61, 1073

Day 175
Word problem: $2478
Money: $649.12
Word problem: $1195
Arithmetic: 1247, 389, $0.54

C.

Day 176
Word problem: 2475 talents
Negative numbers: -89, lost 89 talents
Percent: $9.90, $9.09, $330, $303
Arithmetic: 1241, 477, $0.59

Day 177
Measurement: 3040 miles
Time: 13 hours 46 minutes
Arithmetic: 1016, 178, $0.88, 3102

Day 178
Mixed number: 1 3/10
Equivalent: 8, 7
Word problem: 8/5, 1 3/5
Arithmetic: 1004, 75, $0.26, 4914

Day 179
Fractions: 8 1/7
Fractions: 20/16, 1 4/16, 1 ¼
Arithmetic: 790, 279, $0.26, 1824

Day 180
Money: $867
Money: $392.68
Word problem: 1206 bags of cookies
Arithmetic: 1524, 454, $0.73

D.

Day 171
Fractions: 8/12 = 2/3
Time: 6 hours 53 minutes, 13 hours 25 minutes
Multiply: 143,250
Divide: 22 R 3

Day 172
Fractions: 4/16 = ¼
Multiply: 160,720
Parallel lines: (left column) 0, 2, 2 (right column) 3, 3, 6

Day 173
Fractions: 3 8/9
Multiply fractions: 56/18 = 28/9 = 3 1/9 (9 x 3 = 27 and 28 − 27 = 1)
Measurement: 1600 miles
Word problem: 36 cookies
Multiply: 336,630 (Multiply 687 x 49 and add a zero onto the answer.)

Day 174
Fractions: 133/15 = 8 13/15
Multiply fractions: 15 12/9 = 16 3/9 = 16 1/3
Percent: $7.50
Roman numerals: CMXL, MCDLXV
Divide: 27 R11

Day 175
Divide: 31.926, 3.1926, 0.31926, 0.031926, 0.0031926
Divide: 34
Multiply: 6170

D.

Day 176
Money: $3725.48
Fractions: 6, 6, 8
Word problem: -1174, lost 1174 talents
Percent: $7.80 (You could find ten percent multiply by four and subtract one percent.)
Divide: 52

Day 177
Probability: yellow 2/10 = 1/5, red 3/10, green 5/10 = ½
Word problem: $124, $124, $126
Percent: 50 %
Word problem: 53 talents
Multiply: 178,560

Day 178
Time: 7 hours 41 minutes
Area: one side is 400 because 2400/6 = 400, one length is 20 because 20 x 20 = 400
Multiply: 492,480

Day 179
Divide: 36 R 3
Word problem: 833 bags of cookies
Word problem: 112 people
Subtract: $4.73, $7.19, $0.36

Day 180
Multiply: 425.83, 4258.3 ; 43,583 ; 435,830 ; 4,258,300
Divide: 59 R 3
Multiply: 44,786

Math

1   A: Counting Backwards, Ordinals B: Critical Thinking C: Multiple Addends
2   A: Skip counting by 2, 5, 10 C: Multiplication
3   Time (A: reading digital clocks, AM, PM B: reading analog clocks to the half hour, minutes in an hour and a half hour C: reading every five minutes D: reading to the second)
4   Addition (A: adding to 10 B: adding to 20 C: adding with expanded form and "carrying")
5   Review
6   Multiple Addends D: Multiplication
7   A: Using a hundreds chart B: Multiplication
8   Subtraction C: "borrowing"
9   Area
10   Review
11   Subtraction
12   Dividing
13   Fractions
14   Doubling
15   Review
16   Multiplication
17   Problem Solving
18   Place Value
19   Expanded form
20   Review
21   Adding by place value using expanded form B: "carrying"
22   Symmetry
23   Subtracting by place value
24   Multiplication
25   Review
26-35 Review Weeks
36   Perimeter A: making ten
37   Area
38   Angles
39   Years C: multiplying hundreds by ones D: long division introduction
40   Review
41   Word Problems
42   Coins
43   Fractions
44   Multiplication A: numbers over 100 B: numbers over 1000
45   Review
46   Rounding
47   Estimation
48   Estimation

49	Comparing numbers
50	Review
51	Elapsed Time
52	Negative numbers
53	Using zeros
54	Algebra – Missing Numbers
55	Review
56	Coin values and using coins
57	Make 100 (B: Intro to "borrowing", C: Subtracting Across Zeros)
58	Geometry (coordinate plane), C: Congruent
59	Comparing Fractions (C: fraction arithmetic)
60	Review
61-70	Review Weeks
71	Roman numerals
72	Measuring with a ruler
73	Decimals
74	Fractions/Decimals
75	Review
76	Place Value
77	Multiplication
78	Subtraction
79	Whole numbers, Fractions, B: Mixed Numbers, D: Improper fractions
80	Review
81	C: subtracting from one dollar, D: adding with carrying into dollars
82	A: writing cents with dollar sign B: adding money, writing dollars and cents C: adding with carrying D: multiplying money
83	Multiplication
84	Checking your work
85	Review
86	Money
87	Weight
88	Length
89	Weight
90	Review
91	Arithmetic, subtracting across zeros
92	Percent
93	Fractions
94	Testing
95	Review
96-105	Review Weeks
106	Fractions
107	Elapsed Time
108	Geometry
109	Fractions

Level A
A Mind for Math
Course Description

Through oral lessons, daily written practice, activities, and weekly reviews, students will study along with a parent or teacher to learn the following topics:

*recognizing and using numbers to 1000
*counting by one, two, five, ten, twenty-five
*comparing numbers using < >
*place value
*ordering numbers, ordinals
*horizontal and vertical arithmetic
*finding missing terms
*word problems
*adding multiple addends
*adding and subtracting without borrowing or carrying up to three digits
*adding and subtracting money
*mental arithmetic
*shapes: circle, square, rectangle, cylinder, cube
*perimeter
*telling time and drawing clocks to the hour and half hour
*recognition and value of pennies, nickels, dimes, and quarters
*counting the value of a group of coins
*measuring with a ruler
*math with inches, centimeters, millimeters, ounces, pounds, milligrams, kilograms
*using pictures to describe fractions
*using fractions to describe parts of a whole, parts of a group
* ½, ¼
*comparing fractions
*using drawings and objects to multiply and divide

Level B
A Mind for Math
Course Description

Through oral lessons, daily written practice, activities, and weekly reviews, students will study along with a parent or teacher to learn the following topics:

*recognizing and using numbers to 10,000
*skip counting
*comparing numbers using < >
*place value
*ordering numbers, ordinals
*patterns
*horizontal and vertical arithmetic
*finding missing terms
*word problems, problem solving
*checking answers
*rounding to the nearest ten and hundred
*estimation
*adding multiple addends
*adding and subtracting with borrowing and carrying
*adding and subtracting money
*subtracting with zeros in the minuend
*mental arithmetic
*shapes: circle, square, rectangle, cylinder, cube, circumference, diameter, radius
*perimeter, area
*telling time to the minute, drawing clocks to the quarter hour
*elapsed time
*recognition and value of pennies, nickels, dimes, and quarters
*counting the value of a group of coins
*measuring with a ruler
*math with inches, centimeters, millimeters, ounces, pounds, milligrams, kilograms
*measurements of cups, pints, quarts, gallons
*using pictures to describe fractions
*using fractions to describe parts of a whole, parts of a group
*tenths
*comparing fractions and decimals
*mixed numbers
*adding and subtracting fractions with common denominators
*using drawings and objects to multiply and divide
*multiply by one and zero

Not covered: graphing I suggest doing some just for fun math on Easy Peasy and do days 128 through 135 on Math 2.

Level C
A Mind for Math
Course Description

Through oral lessons, daily written practice, activities, and weekly reviews, students will study along with a parent or teacher to learn the following topics:

*recognizing and using numbers into millions
*skip counting
*comparing numbers using < >
*place value
*patterns
*horizontal and vertical arithmetic
*finding missing terms
*word problems
*problem solving
*rounding and estimation
*checking work
*adding and subtracting with borrowing and carrying
*adding and subtracting money
*subtracting with zeros in the minuend
*mental arithmetic
*shapes: rectangular prism, cylinder, cube, circumference, diameter, radius
*perimeter, area, including area of a triangle
*telling time to the minute
*elapsed time
*counting the value of a group of coins
*measuring with a ruler
*math with inches, centimeters, millimeters, ounces, pounds, milligrams, kilograms,
 meters, yards, feet, kilometers, miles
*measurements of cups, pints, quarts, gallons
*using fractions to describe parts of a whole, parts of a group
*tenths
*comparing fractions and decimals
*equivalent fractions
*mixed numbers, adding mixed numbers with a common denominator
*adding and subtracting fractions with common denominators
*multiplying single, double, and triple digits
*multiplying money
*using objects and pictures to divide

Not covered: graphing I suggest doing some just for fun math on Easy Peasy and do days 171 through 177 on Math 3.

Level D
A Mind for Math
Course Description

Through oral lessons, daily written practice, activities, and weekly reviews, students will study along with a parent or teacher to learn the following topics:

*comparing numbers using < >
*place value
*patterns
*horizontal and vertical arithmetic
*finding missing terms
*word problems
*problem solving
*rounding and estimation
*checking work
*adding and subtracting decimals with borrowing and carrying
*adding and subtracting money
*counting the value of a group of coins
*subtracting with zeros in the minuend
*mental arithmetic
*shapes: rectangular prism, cylinder, cube, circumference, diameter, radius
*perimeter, area, including area of a triangle and pyramid
*telling time to the minute
*elapsed time
*measuring with a ruler
*math with inches, centimeters, millimeters, ounces, pounds, milligrams, kilograms, meters, yards, feet, kilometers, miles
*measurements of cups, pints, quarts, gallons
*tenths
*comparing fractions and decimals
*equivalent fractions
*improper fractions, reducing and simplifying fractions
*mixed numbers, adding and subtracting with an uncommon denominator
*adding and subtracting fractions with uncommon denominators
*multiplying single, double, and triple digits, fractions, decimals
*multiplying and dividing money
*dividing, long division, fractions as division, dividing fractions
*remainders, remainders as fractions
*angles, probability, coordinate plane

Not covered: graphing I suggest doing some just for fun math on Easy Peasy and do days 31 through 34 on Math 4.

Thank you for using the Genesis Curriculum. Hope you had a great year of learning together.

Look for more years of the Genesis Curriculum using both Old and New Testament books of the Bible. Find us online at genesiscurriculum.com to read about the latest developments in this expanding curriculum.

GC Steps are three years of preschool and kindergarten that prepare students in reading, writing, and math. These are aimed at children ages three to six.

GC Math allows students from about first through fourth grade to do their daily math together. Word problems and applications come from the daily Bible reading in the main curriculum. Students all have a leveled workbook to complete.

The Genesis Curriculum Rainbow Readers take quality reading and present them in a new way. Each book stands alone and has a dictionary with the included vocabulary underlined in the text. The books have also been edited to use modern American spelling to help your children spell by knowing what looks right. Some of the books have been lightly edited for content issues. There are also occasional helps with explanations or pictures. They were made with GC students in mind.

Made in the USA
Monee, IL
05 September 2020